" Following the principles presented in *Complete Physique,* with its wholistic approach of strength training, nutrition, supplementation and envisioning helped me achieve my dream of going to the Olympics, and ultimately bringing home the gold!"

> ~ **Emily LeSueur**
> *1996 Olympic Gold Medalist*

"**When I changed my attitude** and began to make the lifestyle changes described in *Complete Physique*, I saw amazing results. I lost 11 percent body fat and 25 pounds in six months. Looking back, I realize it wasn't that hard. It just took making small changes in each of the areas the book teaches. This total program has created a totally new, healthier, happier me!"

> ~ **Wendy Tanner**
> *Mother of six*

" *Complete Physique* **changes the lives** of people in a dramatic and healthful way. *Complete Physique* can mean the 'start of a new tomorrow' for anyone interested in better personal health. I have seen the program work time and time again. Professionally and personally speaking, I fully endorse *Complete Physique* as a means of regaining personal health."

> ~ **Gene A. Charles**
> *Ph.D. (Cellular Nutrition),*
> *M.S. (Microbiology)*

Infinity²'s

Complete Physique
a Program of E.N.E.R.G.Y.

Biochemistry Consultant: Stan Bynum, Ph.D
Editor: Jennifer Hammer, C.CN., C.S.C.S.
Art Director: Tim Peterson
Production Artist: William Alyea

Printed in the United States of America

Produced and manufactured for:
EcoQuest International
Greeneville, TN
under license of
Infinity²
Mesa, AZ

EcoQuest and the EcoQuest Logo are trademarks of EcoQuest International.

Infinity², the Infinity² logo, the Infinity² products mentioned herein are trademarks of Infinity², Inc.

ISBN 09665401-0-7

7024–02010

Infinity²'s

Complete Physique

a Program of E.N.E.R.G.Y.

Infinity² Inc.

Foreword

Complete Physique's Role in Improving the Quality of Life

Complete Physique is at the core of helping people to live healthier lives. This unique blend of true health principles that we discovered and brought together continues to be the flagship and foundation of Infinity². Here, in one easy-to-implement program, is everything an individual needs to adopt a healthier lifestyle and move to optimum levels of well-being.

Table of Contents

How to Use Complete Physique

Complete Physique is a lifestyle program.

No matter how old you are or what your current state of fitness is, *Complete Physique* offers the necessary tools to help you achieve the quality of life that is only possible for those people who have health and vitality.

All you need to do is begin. Follow these simple steps to a healthier life!

1. Browse through *Complete Physique* to get an overview of the program and become familiar with the layout of the book. Then go back and read each of the chapters thoroughly. This will strengthen your foundation and motivate you to stick to the program.

2. Start the *Complete Physique* **Nutrition Plan** as soon as possible. Begin by setting up your kitchen as described in the Nutrition chapter (p. 95). Then, try the delicious recipes and menu suggestions. First and foremost (right now, today!), implement the basics of the nutrition plan by getting rid of all white flour, sugar (replace with fructose), carbonated drinks and high fat items in your house.

3. Begin the *Complete Physique* **Exercise program** outlined in this book (see p.119). Choose three days a week for your resistance exercise workout (e.g., Monday, Wednesday and Friday; or Tuesday, Thursday and Saturday) and set aside approximately 20 minutes on each of those days; then, using the pictures and descriptions in the Exercise chapter, perform the outlined exercises. This section of the book teaches you how to adapt each exercise to fit your particular needs. On the alternating three days, participate in a cardiovasular activity as described in the Exercise chapter. Rest on the seventh day.

4. **Replenish the nutrients you need** by taking the supplements as recommended on the labels and in the Replenishment chapter. Before you begin, complete the "How Much Do I Need?" questionnaire found on page 156 to determine your specific replenishment requirements. Retake the questionnaire monthly. You should notice that your need for replenishment decreases as your lifestyle improves.

5. **Stick to the complete program.** Even if you start slowly, consistency is the key. Incorporate at least one of the suggestions from each area of the program (Envision, Nutrition, Exercise and Replenishment) and then, stick to it. Throughout the book you will find suggestions for maintaining your progress.

6. **Enjoy yourself!** *Complete Physique* is a lifestyle that is exhilarating. It will give you the health and the energy to truly enjoy life and to experience the very best that life has to offer. What more could you want?

Chapter One

Complete Physique

A Program of E.N.E.R.G.Y.

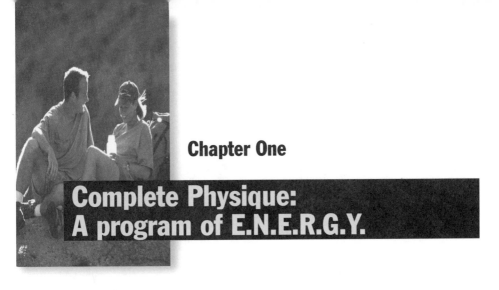

Chapter One

Complete Physique:
A program of E.N.E.R.G.Y.

Health Is Pivotal

Money is important. But without health, we can't work to earn the money we need. Without health, we cannot use our money to do the things we enjoy.

Time is also important. But without health, we cannot spend our time the way we want. If we are sick or in ill-health, our time is no longer our own.

Think about every aspect of life. Family, for example. How can you be a fully contributing family member or enjoy spending time with your family if you are not healthy and full of energy?

Perhaps you want to be a leader in your community or at work. Perhaps you want to travel the world. Maybe you have a sport you want to perfect or a hobby you want to immerse yourself in. You may value dance or music or another creative or artistic activity. Whatever it is that you prize most in your life, your health has a direct impact on your ability to become fully involved in and get the most from that activity.

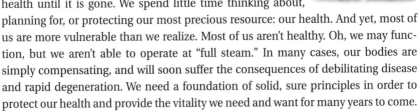

Unfortunately, many people are unconcerned about health until it is gone. We spend little time thinking about, planning for, or protecting our most precious resource: our health. And yet, most of us are more vulnerable than we realize. Most of us aren't healthy. Oh, we may function, but we aren't able to operate at "full steam." In many cases, our bodies are simply compensating, and will soon suffer the consequences of debilitating disease and rapid degeneration. We need a foundation of solid, sure principles in order to protect our health and provide the vitality we need and want for many years to come.

See if any of these examples of real people sound like you:

> **Kathy, a successful businesswoman,** had created a small chain of fast-food restaurants. Her family had never been closer, money had never been easier to come by. Kathy's dream had come true. Except for one problem, Kathy's health was failing. She was in her early 40s, but the stress and demands of the restaurants seemed to sap her strength and energy. Kathy didn't have the stamina to enjoy her dream.

Martin was a law student with a wife and three children when the stresses of law school, along with his poor eating habits, began to negatively affect his health. He gained weight and developed stomach ulcers that kept him in constant pain. Medications and doctor bills cost him a small fortune. He was often tired and irritable, and he no longer had the energy to spend much time with his family.

Cynthia had already achieved great success in the Women's National Basketball Association being voted MVP for three consecutive Championship games. In order to continue playing at her peak performance, Cynthia knew it was vital to maintain a strong body and optimal health. She began her search for products and protocols that would enable her to achieve these goals.

Theresa, a young mother of five, was lethargic and depressed. She had leg cramps and was often bloated. No matter how she tried, she couldn't seem to lose the extra twelve pounds she had gained with her last pregnancy.

Ana, a ninety-eight-year-old woman, had fallen and broken her hip. The hip seemed to have healed, but her muscle strength had deteriorated.

Stan, a business man, had planned a vacation to the beach. He and his wife were going to be spending the week with two couples they had gone to high school with fifteen years previously. He wanted to trim down enough to fit into his 34-inch-waist pants before their trip.

Although none of these people may have had dramatic wake-up calls, whether they realized it or not, in one way or another, their health was failing. And, so is yours.

Regardless of how healthy you may now look and feel, if you live in an industrialized country, your good health is being bombarded and eroded at a much quicker pace than necessary.

Fortunately specific, concrete, accurate answers are available. These answers aren't just quick-fix ideas. They are the principles we need to apply as the long-term lifestyle practices that keep us healthy. They are the answers that virtually every individual needs.

The answers we discovered make up the *Complete Physique* program which has yielded results for thousands of individuals like the people we mentioned earlier.

Here are the results they were able to achieve with *Complete Physique*:

Kathy says *Complete Physique* **has reduced her stress** significantly, enabling her to be more productive and more efficient.

Martin has been free from any problems with ulcers for several years. His wife says he's like the man she married all over again.

Chapter One: Complete Physique – a Program of E.N.E.R.G.Y.

Cynthia has achieved the results she was looking for with Infinity²'s products. Her confidence in the company, its products and its vision is evidenced by her willingness to speak publicly in support of Infinity².

Theresa lost 20 pounds and reduced her body fat by 9 percent.

Ana began walking on her own and caring for herself again.

And, Stan reached his goal and wore the 34-inch-waist pants on vacation.

It may seem far-fetched to claim that we all need the same approach to health. We are a society that has a different pill or product for every ailment. Take this for a headache; take this to cure back pain; take this to fix a swollen right toe.

> *Complete Physique is the only system available that provides everything you need for total health and fitness.*

Plus, fitness varies from one individual to another. Some people are very sick, others have a healthy, active life. So how can we say that the solution to every individual's health challenges is essentially the same?

Returning to a Balanced State

The solution is the same because the problem is virtually the same. We are out of balance. At times we get out of balance quickly, yet most of us lose the vital, internal balance more slowly, almost imperceptibly as we make unhealthy choices day after day.

Returning to a balanced state to what we call "homeostasis" requires a complete program with the same elements for each of us — regardless of our state of health. Granted, some people may need to modify the elements a little and may need additional support at first, but the key to optimum health for each of us is a wholistic program.

In your search for answers about healthy friends and family may have offered well-intentioned advice in the form of the latest magazine articles or a "hot" new audio tape. Watching television programs, reading books and consulting with doctors and supposed specialists often just lead to a mass of confusion and contradiction.

Before becoming extremely discouraged with it all, try creating a vision, a clear mental picture of the kind of health you want. Such a vision will lead you to the truth. Vision will help you see what you really want: energy, vitality, true health. Of course, this takes a complete program for a total style of living.

Health Requires a Wholistic Approach

To find such a complete program, we began to search out the individuals who were the experts, those who had actually done the research. We found that answers were indeed available. Top scientists and researchers in the field of nutrition had verified these answers time and time again. Most exciting of all, these research-proven principles were the same as those found by looking to the laws of nature. Science also verified that a complete program was the key to returning to homeostasis.

Nowhere, however, was such a program available. Programs offered by some supplement companies hinted at what was necessary but said little more than "eat right" and "exercise." They promoted their own pet principle or favorite fad, but none of them provided the necessary education, guidelines and tools that would help people obtain the end results of feeling and looking great.

Diet centers and gyms offered programs which focused only on weight loss on building large muscles. As far as health goes, their approach was incomplete.

By working with the experts, we were able to bring together all of the necessary elements to create a unique, comprehensive program for health. This program — *Complete Physique* — was first implemented in a small fitness and health center called Infinity² Fitness Center. Infinity² Fitness Center was not located in a prestigious or high-traffic area, and we did no advertising. Yet, within two years we had conducted over 15,000 training sessions for people from all walks of life including professional athletes, rehabilitation clients, busy professionals, businessmen and women, teenagers and housewives.

The same principles used in the Infinity² Fitness Center were soon published in book form, making it possible for thousands of others to use this complete lifestyle program.

Long-Term Benefits

The results have been phenomenal, and most exciting of all, they are lasting. People don't quickly lose weight and then even more quickly put it back on. They don't take a "vitamin" and feel a burst of energy that lasts only for a short time. Instead, they experience long-term results and you will to. You will be able to:

- **Burn fat** more efficiently
- **Increase** the number of calories you burn
- **Reshape** and sculpt your body
- **Improve** your overall health and well-being
- **Increase** your energy levels and your satisfaction with life
- **Think** more clearly and remember more
- **Increase** your ability to resist disease
- **Ward off** depression and mood swings
- **Look great**, feel great and live longer

These benefits and more can result from balancing your body using the *Complete Physique* program. This program takes a thorough, wholistic approach. It's a combination of simple, effective elements that are best explained using the acronym E.N.E.R.G.Y.™

The E.N.E.R.G.Y. acronym stands for:

Envision — *Complete Physique* documents the importance of visualization and teaches you how to create a mental picture that will enable you to reach your health and fitness goals.

Nutrition — This program provides everything you need for healthful eating: shopping how-tos, menus and recipes, guidelines for eating out and directions for setting up a *Complete Physique* kitchen.

Exercise — With the *Complete Physique* program you will be instructed in the proper, most effective way to exercise. This includes an exercise routine that you can do at home along with pictures and instructions to follow and charts to track your progress.

Replenishment — This total system defines everyone's need to replace nutrients that are lost because of environmental factors. It also discusses the best products to meet those needs. **Best of all, you will learn how to take fewer of these products as your lifestyle improves.**

Generates — Applying the proven principles found in *Complete Physique* will generate amazing benefits. Best of all, it will produce...

You! — At last, a truly complete program that will yield the healthier, happier "you" that you desire.

With *Complete Physique* you will feel as if you have a whole new lease on life. Your body will return to balance and will function more efficiently, more optimally than it has for some time (possibly for years). Remember the examples we presented at the beginning of this chapter? Wouldn't you like to have a similar success story to tell?

As you apply the principles presented in *Complete Physique*, you, too, will have such a story. You will learn like we did and like thousands of others have that health is a precious possession. And, you'll wonder how you could have gone so long without it.

Do I Need?

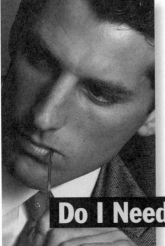

Chapter Two

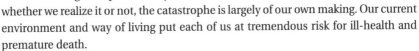
Do I Need?

If an airplane crashes, the tragedy hits us all with shock and emotion; and thousands of man-hours are spent to determine the cause.

If an earthquake destroys several city blocks, we listen intently as the media conducts a major campaign to point out ways that lives could have been spared.

Yet, in the United States alone 1.5 million people die every year — not from old-age, but from largely preventable diseases — and that tragedy is virtually ignored.

Accidents and natural disasters undoubtedly deserve the scrutiny they receive. Unfortunately, we have become callous to the less-sensational losses that occur every day. Lives are being lost prematurely and unnecessarily. And, whether we realize it or not, the catastrophe is largely of our own making. Our current environment and way of living put each of us at tremendous risk for ill-health and premature death.

However, the good news is that all can be changed. By employing the right techniques and making even small alterations in our lifestyle and our surroundings, we can ward off the impending catastrophe. While the alterations don't have to be dramatic, they do need to be based on correct principles. By following the proven guidelines in *Complete Physique*, you will find the adage to be true that small changes create profound outcomes.

The question we must all answer is "Do I Need? Do I need to supplement? Do I need to exercise? Do I need to do anything to improve my health?"

Differing Opinions Mask the Truth

Each of us faces a similar dilemma. What do we need for health today? Thousands of differing opinions confront us daily. Magazines, infomercials and billboards bombard us with the latest health developments and nutrition crazes. This information overload has made the truth harder to find.

The problem is more grave than many of us realize. Studies show that we can no longer rely on the "traditional" sources that we have sought for guidance. Often the nutrition recommendations come from companies that are merely trying to market their own product. Weight loss counselors and coaches are often misinformed. Even doctors have little education in the area of nutrition and preventive medicine; and their help often comes too late, after our health is gone.

Special Interest Groups Have Their Own Interests in Mind

Evidence also reveals that special interest groups apparently have only their own interests in mind. Research has exposed extensive cover-ups by groups that we thought we could trust for health advice. For example, the American Dietitians Association (ADA), a 65,000-member organization, has provided public education and has helped set nutritional guidelines for schools and hospitals. Yet, the ADA receives substantial contributions from groups like the National Livestock and Meat Board and the Sugar Association and from companies like M&M Mars, McDonald's and Coca-Cola.[1] Do you suppose those contributions may influence what is being promoted as "good nutrition"?

Another eye-opening example comes from recent investigations into the traditional teachings of the American Heart Association and other organizations. For years we have been told that coronary heart disease is primarily linked to high intake of saturated fat and cholesterol. Yet, researcher Dr. George Mann states that this "has been repeatedly shown to be wrong, yet, ... continues to be exploited by scientists, fund-raising enterprises, food companies, and even governmental agencies. The public is being deceived by the greatest health scam of the century."[2]*

Our Health Is Lost in the Shuffle

We have been lulled into a false sense of security. Even the most health-conscious individuals seem to believe that if a package or ad contains the word "health," it must be healthy for us. We overlook the fact that health has become a multi-billion dollar industry. In 1995, over $940 billion was spent on health care in the United States alone.[3] While competition for our money rages on, our health gets lost in the shuffle.

How healthy are we? Modern medicine and technology have lengthened the average lifespan; yet, what about the quality of that life? Employees miss more time from work, hospital stays are more frequent and patient loads at nursing homes have increased. Chronic diseases like arthritis and heart disease are more prevalent than ever and these diseases set in at an earlier age. Today we are four times as likely to have a chronic disease by age 40 than was the case only 20 years ago.[4]

Too many of us are struggling to pay increasing health care costs. Too many of us are robbed of the time and energy we need to enjoy life. We should be outraged. With our own health and the well-being of our family and friends

---

*Saturated fat is only part of the cause of heart disease and only a small percentage of the population is sensitive to dietary cholesterol intake.

on the line, we should each want to know "Do I need to take supplements? Do I need to exercise? What steps do I need to take to improve my health now so I can enjoy life in the coming years?"

Sorting It Out

During our search for overall health, we became determined to sort out the differing opinions and unfounded claims and to find the answers that were backed by research. We wanted proof. We didn't have the time or the money to be led on a wild chase. We wanted to get healthy.

We discovered that many other people were in the same situation. Some were sick or in pain, and they didn't know where to turn. Many others were concerned about subtle changes in their health, and they wanted to reverse the decline; but they seemed to think it was inevitable.

Ill-Health Isn't Inevitable

By studying the research and going to the experts we found that ill-health is far from inevitable. Every individual can experience profound health improvements and can extend the length and the quality of his or her life by incorporating a wholistic lifestyle program.

During the past six years as we have worked closely with health care practitioners, we have seen over and over that individuals who are under a doctor's care need a wholistic program to support healing. In fact, today over 5,000 health care practitioners use the *Complete Physique* program in their clinics to provide a foundation for their patients' healing.

We have also consulted with athletes at every level, in virtually every sport — from professional baseball, basketball and football players, to Olympic wrestler's and swimmers, to college and high school track stars. Each of these athletes needs the same kind of foundation before they can improve. Sure, they can continue to do drills and workouts, but without a foundational wellness program, those drills are practically useless. Improved performance cannot come to an athlete or to any other individual, whose health is out of balance. In essence, that person is sick and will remain so until balance or what is known as homeostasis, is restored. Improved performance is only possible if an individual follows a solid program for overall wellness and then builds upon those underlying principles.

The same holds true for "couch potatoes" who want to begin a program of health, or for extremely active individuals who want to stay healthy. It takes a foundation of sound, basic principles to bring health into balance and keep it that way.

In our determination to spread health we wanted to create programs that were based on need and backed by research and that were easy to apply in today's world.

Complete Physique is such a program. The result of a thorough investigation into our current health catastrophe, it is a wholistic lifestyle program that addresses the health needs of virtually every individual.

We call *Complete Physique* a program of E.N.E.R.G.Y. and use that acronym to outline the elements that are essential for health — Envision, Nutrition, Exercise and Replenishment Generate You!

This unique program includes guidelines to help you quickly get started and tracking systems to keep you motivated. It answers the questions "Do I Need...?" and explains how to meet the identified needs. In short, *Complete Physique* provides E.N.E.R.G.Y.

Do I Need to Envision?

The first "E" in the acronym E.N.E.R.G.Y. represents "Envision." We have discovered that envisioning makes a difference. Any achievement, even an action as routine as going up a flight of stairs or driving to the corner grocery store, is envisioned before it is enacted.

The mind has an amazing capacity to direct the body.

In professional sports "mind training" has been used for years. For example, "In 1976 the U.S. Olympic ski team, before making difficult downhill runs, would rehearse the entire run in their imaginations, thinking of each bump and turn and how they would cope with it. They turned better runs than they ever had before, and the United States won some surprising medals."[5]

Patients who have employed visualization have experienced remarkable, almost miraculous, instances of healing. Using mental imagery we can literally influence bodily processes. For instance, studies have shown that individuals can exert "voluntary control over blood flow in certain areas of the body."[6]

Visualization Drives Accomplishment

Through the years successful business people have learned to use visualization to drive their accomplishments. And whether you realize it or not, your vision (or lack thereof) is at the root of what you have achieved in life. Each of us envisions, but since much of this mental imaging is done subconsciously, we often take no notice of it; few of us learn to access it and use it to our advantage.

Yet, your accomplishments and achievements and particularly your current health and fitness level are largely due to your own mental images. Have you ever said something like, "I just don't *see* myself running a marathon." "I can't *imagine* being pain free," or "I can't *picture* myself wearing a swimsuit again"?

The verbs in those statements — "see, imagine and "picture" — all refer to the mental imaging that is critical in any achievement. To change your present state of health or to preserve the good health you now have, you must create a clear mental

ANALYSIS REPORT

SUBJECT STATUS: HOMEOSTATIC

SUBJECT ENJOYS GOOD HEALTH, VITALITY, ENERGY AND SOUND STATE OF MIND.

SUBJECT PRACTICES ENVISIONING

SUBJECT EATS MANY RAW FOODS SUBJECT AVOIDS SUGAR, WHITE FLOUR, ALCOHOL AND CARBONATED DRINKS.

SUBJECT STRENGTH TRAINS REGULARLY.

SUBJECT REPLENISHES ENZYMES, VITAMINS, MINERALS, ANTIOXIDANTS, CHROMIUM AND FLORA.

picture of what health "looks like" to you. If you don't "see" good health, you will never achieve it.

When we applied the research and made this technique part of our total training program, we found that vision made the difference between success and failure time after time.

Harness the Power to Succeed

We are convinced (and the research bears this out) that, regardless of whatever else you may do for health, in order to succeed you must harness the power of visualization. "You become what you think about all day," and you can direct your thoughts so you can accomplish the things you desire most. Without a clear vision of health, you will very likely end up with the sickness and disease facing most people today. Rather than passively allowing advertisements and media blitzes to program your mental images, you can actively formulate your own visions and thus, take control of the outcome.

In recent years much has been written about visualization and the theories behind this practice. Based on these proven theories, *Complete Physique* offers a simple, effective way for you to put vision into practice. With the technique outlined in the Envision chapter, you will discover how to "envision" your health goal in such a way that you will assuredly be led to achieve it.

Do I Need Nutrition?

The "N" in the E.N.E.R.G.Y. acronym represents "Nutrition." Nutrition has been defined as the "act or process of nourishing." In other words, a food is nutritious if it supplies the nutrients the body needs "to promote growth, repair and vital processes." The basic purpose of nutrition is to keep us alive, but even more importantly, nutrition provides what the body needs for energy and day-to-day functioning.

In today's fast-paced world, few of us receive the nutrition we need. Even though much of what we eat is promoted as nutritious, in reality, the way we eat shortens our life and destroys the quality of our life in the process!

Corporate America has keyed-in to the renewed public interest about nutrition. Advertising agencies and the media recognize that there is a growing concern about healthy eating. We see and hear commercials that highlight products "for moms who care about their family's health," or "for the active individual." Fast-food restaurants have jumped on the bandwagon and have published their "health facts."

Caution: Your Choice of Food May Be Fatal

Unfortunately, what is currently touted as nutritious often doesn't provide the nutrition the body needs. Our "food" is often so highly processed and chemically altered that it no longer promotes healthy function. If the "fortified," "enriched," "nutritious" foods we eat nourish our bodies as advertisers claim, why is it that eight out of ten of the leading causes of death in North America today are nutrition-related?[7] Did you know you are five times as likely to die from what you eat than from any other cause? In other words, your choice of food may be more deadly than cigarettes, automobile accidents or natural calamities.

The highly processed foods that most of us eat every day are stripped of natural vitamins, minerals and enzymes and are filled with chemical additives and preservatives. Even the foods we prepare at home are often pre-packaged mixes or ready-to-eat meals with most of the nutrients cooked away. These "convenience foods" are proving to be a very convenient way to end up with ill-health and a shortened lifespan. In essence, we are committing slow-but-sure suicide every time we eat a modern meal.

"Convenient" Ill-health

Over 35 years ago, Dr. Francis Marion Pottenger, Jr. chronicled the effects of heat-processed foods. His ten-year study found that cats that ate raw meat and milk survived operations better, were more vigorous, had better overall health and had healthier offspring. Cats that ate cooked foods had increased "heart problems;... underactivity of the thyroid...; infections of the kidney, liver...and bladder; arthritis and inflammation of the joints;"[8] and other problems.

Pottenger found the same to be true for humans. "Observation of our young people reveals that humans are subjected to the same food deficiencies as are seen in The Cat Study,"[9] Pottenger says. "We are burying our heads in the sand and ignoring the fact that our modern methods of production may be rendering valuable foods dangerous."[10]

Processed foods continue to rise in popularity with more fast-food restaurants and more packaged meals available. In an assessment of modern eating habits, statistics showed that for men aged 23 to 34, one out of every three meals is eaten away from home. (In this survey, "away from home" meant at a restaurant or fast-food establishment. It did not include brown-bag lunches or meals that were prepared in their own kitchens and then eaten away from home.)[11]

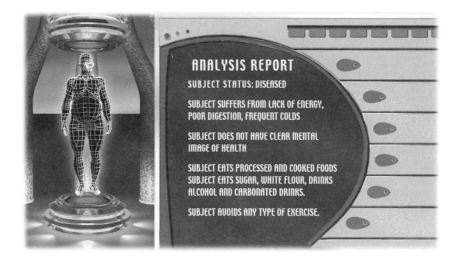

ANALYSIS REPORT

SUBJECT STATUS: DISEASED

SUBJECT SUFFERS FROM LACK OF ENERGY,
POOR DIGESTION, FREQUENT COLDS

SUBJECT DOES NOT HAVE CLEAR MENTAL
IMAGE OF HEALTH

SUBJECT EATS PROCESSED AND COOKED FOODS
SUBJECT EATS SUGAR, WHITE FLOUR, DRINKS
ALCOHOL AND CARBONATED DRINKS.

SUBJECT AVOIDS ANY TYPE OF EXERCISE.

Evidence shows nutrition trends are creating widespread health problems. Well-known nutritionist Royal Lee wrote, "We know that people who have the best health in this world are those who use the least of our so-called civilized foods, such as white flour, refined sugar, soft drinks and hard drinks and the multiplicity of packaged and canned groceries."[12] Lee spoke out particularly against white flour, pointing out that in 1953, the *A.M.A. Journal* associated "acute poisoning" and "morose depression" with both kinds of flour bleach commonly used.[13] Although mental disturbances, severe itch, loss of appetite, insomnia, diabetes and heart disease have all been linked to white flour, it continues to be marketed and even promoted as healthy.

*Mis*information Superhighway

Sadly, although we may recognize the need for nutrition, we are enticed by many falsehoods. As we mentioned earlier, heart disease — the number one killer today — has been blamed on "dietary saturated fat and cholesterol." Recently, *Consumers' Research* magazine said this is a "health scam," and that heart disease is "not what you think." Instead, heart disease is linked to "devitalized" or "fabricated" foods, including refined sugar, pasteurized milk, soft drinks, fortified white flour, imitation broth products, egg powders and even synthetic vitamins.[14]

Again, a recent *New York Times* article, divulged that the American Dietetic Association(ADA) is largely funded by trade groups and food companies. The article says the ADA takes the "wishy-washy stance" that there are not "good or bad foods," because they rely on industry money which "means that they never criticize the food industry." [15]

As far as nutrition goes, it seems we are in the middle of a "*mis*information" superhighway. This misinformation is taking its toll. A ten State Nutrition Survey concluded that "a significant proportion of the population (was) malnourished or was at high risk of developing nutritional problems."[16]

Only one person in eight eats enough fruit or vegetables to meet the guidelines established by the U.S. government.[17] In fact, it is estimated that "30 to 33 percent of our total adult caloric intake is being derived from sources of no nutritional value..."[18]

Running on Empty

Just as a car must have fuel and proper upkeep, your body must have high quality food to function correctly. Every cell of your body is either healthy or sick depending on the food you eat. The body must be fueled with foods that are nutrient dense and as close to their natural state as possible so nutrients can be delivered to the individual cells of the body where they can be used to keep the cells healthy. If you aren't eating nutritious food, what reserves do you suppose your body is drawing from? You may be able to "run" for a while, but you will soon "break down."

The good news is that balanced nutrition, as outlined in this book, yields almost immediate benefits. Proper nutrition promotes optimum organ function, energy production and increased resistance to disease and aging. It's really quite simple: to feel well, eat well. To live well and long, eat well.

The answer to "Do I need nutrition?" is most definitely, "Yes." However, to escape the current downward spiral, we need more than hype and headlines. We need to be nourished, not just fed. That requires a systematic approach that is not only effective but is also easy to implement. *Complete Physique* provides such an approach.

Like many people, you may have made attempts to eat more nutritiously. However, as pointed out above, you may have been led astray or perhaps found it was time-consuming to eat what you thought were balanced meals. Wouldn't it be great to have specific, easy-to-follow guidelines that would allow you to escape the food fads and avoid the confusion that reigns in the area of nutrition?

That's exactly what you'll find in the Nutrition chapter of this book. *Complete Physique* outlines a comprehensive plan that will fit perfectly with your busy lifestyle. You will still be able to eat fast foods. You will still be able to eat at your favorite restaurants. You will be able to set up your kitchen so cooking at home can be simple and healthy. You will find menus, recipes and shopping tips and the "whys" behind the recommended food choices. This system makes nutritious eating so uncomplicated that you will have no reason to fall back into old, unhealthy habits. *Complete Physique*'s Nutrition Plan is beneficial, enjoyable and delicious!

Do I Need Exercise?

The second "E" in the E.N.E.R.G.Y. acronym represents "Exercise." Exercise may not be your favorite topic. Mentioning the word may bring to mind memories of sore muscles, expensive gym memberships and useless mail-order gimmicks. It conjures up remembrances of pain and hard work and reminds you that the last exercise program you tried occupied too much time and didn't furnish results. Besides, you've heard so many conflicting opinions about exercise that you hardly know where to begin. You may wonder, "Who needs exercise anyway?"

The answer is "We all do." But let me assure you, it's not what you may be thinking. There is a way to exercise that is so effective, and takes so little time that you will be amazed. Results will keep you motivated and you will feel better than you ever have!

As with nutrition, there has been a great deal of misinformation published about exercise. Ads push the latest gadgets, exercise video's and workout apparel but don't tell us how to exercise correctly. Overwhelmed and discouraged, many people have decided that exercise is not for them. Still others are needlessly expending energy and money on programs that aren't helpful.

Hazardous Habits

The past decade saw a surge of interest in physical activity, but that is waning and giving way to more sedentary lifestyles. According to the 1996 U.S. Surgeon General's Report entitled *Physical Activity and Health,* more than 60 percent of adults don't participate in even moderate physical activity on a daily basis, and one out of every four people is completely inactive.[19] Another study estimated that over 92 percent of the population is physically unfit.[20]

This widespread inactivity contributes to premature death and unnecessary illness for millions of people each year.[21] Think of it, millions of people — not hundreds, but millions — die unnecessarily each year because of inactivity.

On the other hand, study after study has demonstrated that physical fitness can generate remarkable health benefits. The largest fitness study ever conducted was reported in the *Journal of the American Medical Association* in 1989. The study measured the fitness levels of 13,344 men and women and then closely monitored them for eight years. Death rates were much lower for the people who were the most physically fit.[22]

Exercise Elevates Health

The study concluded, "Higher levels of physical fitness were beneficial, even in subjects with other risk factors such as high blood pressure, elevated cholesterol, cigarette smoking and a family history of heart disease." It appears that fitness compensates for risk factors that might otherwise shorten life. "Unfit people without any risk factors had a higher risk of dying than fit people with all the major risk factors."[23]

The 1996 U.S. Surgeon General's Report mentioned above is an in-depth, thoroughly documented treatise on the benefits of physical activity. It states moderate exercise can ward off afflictions such as cardiovascular disease, colon cancer, adult-onset diabetes, osteoporosis and depression. For example, the Report cites a five-year study of 10,000 American men ages 20 to 82 which concluded, "Those who improved their fitness through exercise had a 64-percent reduction in death from cardiovascular disease compared with those who remained unfit."[24]

Many people have avoided cigarette smoking because they recognize the dangers of heart disease and cancer. Did you know that the risk of getting heart disease and cancer is even greater for sedentary individuals than for those who smoke?[25]

Additional Benefits

Exercise reduces low back pain, headaches and digestive problems. Studies show that eighty percent of all low back pain is due to weak abdominal muscles.

Insufficient exercise often brings on arthritis and osteoporosis. Osteoporosis strikes eight out of ten women. Yet, according to research, that number could be greatly reduced if women would do muscle-strengthening exercises. A study reported in *The Lancet*, a British medical journal, showed that the rate of bone loss is significantly greater in women today than it was two centuries ago. The study concluded that the major difference is that 18th and 19th Century women engaged in more physical activity than their modern counterparts.

Exercise reduces the harmful effects of stress, increases mental and physical energy, and boosts self-esteem. A person who exercises has a much greater ability to lose body fat, as well. In a 10 year study, diet centers that do not recommend exercise showed an average weight *gain* of four pounds per person.[26] Research also shows that weight lost through dieting without exercise often comes from muscles, organs and fluids, not from body fat.

With the overwhelming evidence to support the need, why are we more sedentary and less fit than ever? The Surgeon General's Report says the decline in activity stems from the fact that people have become confused by the many options and the misinformation. We agree. In addition, we think many people have either tried an ineffective program, or have done the exercises wrong; and when they didn't get results, they became discouraged and quit.

In *Complete Physique*, you will find an exercise plan that will allow you to derive the greatest benefits in the shortest amount of time. It is a program that includes both "moderate activity" and "resistance exercise" as recommended by the Surgeon General's Report. By examining the available research and conducting studies of our own, we have been able to develop this quick, effective program.

Strength Training for Health

The *Complete Physique* plan emphasizes strength training (resistance exercises) as a foundation because research conclusively demonstrates the health benefits associated with this technique. The Exercise chapter also teaches how to derive cardiovascular benefits by properly including cardiovascular exercise in your overall fitness program.

Strength training offers benefits for every individual. In his book, *Strength Fitness*, Wayne Westcott states, "Sensible strength training can benefit just about everyone with regard to physical capacity, metabolic function, athletic power, injury prevention and physical appearance."[27] In addition, Westcott says, "Most men and women have no idea that unless they perform regular strength exercise they lose approximately five pounds of muscle every ten years. Neither do they understand that this steady loss of muscle is largely responsible for lowering their metabolic rate by 5 percent every decade."[28]

Strength training has been proven to:

- **Increase** basal metabolic rate so more calories are burned even when you're not exercising

- **Decrease** body fat percentage

- **Improve** the shape of the body

- **Provide** cardiovascular benefits

- **Boost** energy levels

- **Reduce** low back pain

- **Provide** added protection against osteoporosis

- **Enhance** overall health and well-being

One of the greatest benefits is the "triple" effect on calorie burning that comes from strength training. First, strength training burns calories during the workout. Then, more calories are burned when the muscles are recuperating and rebuilding during the 24 hours following a workout. Third, strength training produces more muscle tissue; and since muscle tissue requires more calories, your metabolism is higher even when you are resting. With strength training your body burns more calories even while you're sleeping.

Strength training results in an increase of *lean* muscle, resulting in the hourglass shape for women and the V-taper shape for men. This is ultimately what people want to accomplish when they diet, but it is impossible to do it through dieting alone.

The quality of your figure is determined to a great extent by your muscle-to-fat ratio, not by your weight. When you gain muscle you get leaner in the sense that your body fat becomes a lower percentage of your overall weight. Thus, when you lose fat and gain muscle, even though your weight may remain the same, the overall change in body composition and physical appearance can be astounding.

Avoid Abusing Cardiovascular Exercise

The benefits of cardiovascular (aerobic) exercise have been highly publicized. Yet, the aerobic craze has produced a great deal of misinformation and faulty programs. Common side effects of improperly performed aerobic exercise include muscle loss, organ damage and eating disorders. There is also an increased risk of injury when participating in aerobic activities.

These problems most often stem from misuse. Most people do cardiovascular exercise to burn fat. However, they often exercise at a much higher level than necessary, which makes the body burn calories from carbohydrates, not fat.

People who do aerobic exercise to lose body fat may see initial results, and, to progress, they think they must continue to exercise longer or harder. However, just adding more time or intensity only increases the incidence of injuries and still does not burn fat. Thus, intense cardiovascular exercise has been linked to degeneration of the joints, especially the back, knees and hips; to states of depression; and to anorexia, bulimia and other obsessive psychological problems.

"This is one of the most important areas as far as exercise education is concerned," says exercise physiologist, Paul Robbins. "We need to teach individuals how to derive benefit from aerobics without overdoing it. Interval training, which changes from high to low intensity is the most productive and safe way to train."

Increase the Fat-Burning Potential

In *Complete Physique*, we recommend moderation when performing aerobic exercise, as indicated in the Exercise chapter. Also, as a result of a recent discovery, we recommend that you take a lipase/chromium supplement to further increase the fat-burning benefit of cardiovascular exercise.

This breakthrough came as a result of a recent study in which an exercise physiologist tested 45 people with a special machine called a metabolic cart. The machine measures Respiratory Exchange Ratio (RER) which indicates whether the body is burning fat or carbohydrates during exercise. The RER test indicated that most people had to stay at a low heart rate (much lower than the rate at which most people do aerobics) in order to burn fat. However, when those people were given a product containing specific fat digesters and other supporting nutrients[1], within 30 minutes they were able to exercise at a higher heart rate and still burn mostly fat. By aiding the body's fat digesting capabilities, exercisers can achieve the benefits they have wanted from aerobics. This amazing breakthrough will impact the exercise industry worldwide and will give aerobics the facelift it has needed to be able to consistently deliver results.

Proven Plan

How would you like to be able to achieve the many benefits of cardiovascular exercise and strength training in as little as two hours a week, exercising in your own home? You can. You don't need fancy gadgets or expensive equipment. All you need to do is follow the simple workout found in the Exercise chapter of this book for 20 minutes, three days a week, and participate in moderate aerobic exercise as outlined for 20 minutes on each of the other three days.

The *Complete Physique* workout program can readily be adapted to fit your present fitness level, in order to help you achieve your fitness goals. Whether you are just starting a fitness program or are already very active, it's a proven program that has demonstrated high effectiveness and compliance. In other words, people who begin this program quickly see results and find they can stick with the program for long-term benefits. Exercising has never been easier or more healthful. There is no other strength training or cardiovascular plan that can produce the kind of results this can in such a short amount of time. The Exercise chapter outlines the programs for you and provides complete instructions, including pictures and a workout chart.

Do I Need Replenishment?

The next letter in the acronym E.N.E.R.G.Y., the "R," represents "Replenishment."

Replenishment, or what is typically called supplementation, has become a controversial subject. One faction says supplementation is pointless and harmful. Another camp claims we need a supplement for every condition and every body part. What's the right answer? Do we need replenishment?

You've seen pictures of starving children with swollen stomachs and emaciated eyes; but you probably think you are immune to something so obviously devastating. It may be true that your caloric intake is sufficient and you're not starving; but there is a good chance that you are deficient in one nutrient or another. In fact, your body may be sounding the alarm but you haven't yet recognized the cause.

For example, perhaps you have noticed some of these things:

Steve's joints were swollen and painful and he had another new bruise on his shin. He was craving chocolate, but he knew a candy bar wouldn't agree with him; his digestion seemed overly sensitive lately. He was taking an antibiotic for the second ear infection he'd had in less than a month. When he brushed his teeth, he noticed that his gums were bleeding and they looked raw.

Steve wasn't alarmed by any of this. He thought he was eating a balanced diet and taking good care of himself. Besides, all he noticed was a few aches and pains, a bruise or two, bleeding gums and an upset stomach. What he didn't see was that these symptoms meant he was deficient in vitamin C. Nor did he know that until this deficiency was corrected, he would continue to get infections and was even at increased risk for a stroke.

Perhaps you're more like Sheila:

Sheila's face had broken out again. She noticed an increase in body odor and bad breath. She constantly had heartburn, and she felt bloated every time she ate even if it was just a snack. She took antacids by the handfuls. Headaches seemed inevitable lately. Looking in the mirror, Sheila thought her lips looked puffy and she wondered what was causing the dark bags under her eyes. She avoided fat and sugar in her diet and exercised faithfully. She couldn't imagine what was wrong.

Sheila was deficient in digestive enzymes. You may have similar symptoms or a host of other indications if you are enzyme deficient. Often these symptoms are linked to the improper digestion that occurs when enzymes are not available including heartburn, gas, nausea, burping, abdominal pain, cramps, diarrhea or constipation.

Enzyme deficiency can also result in mental fatigue (especially after a meal), lack of concentration, memory loss and nervousness as well as insomnia or nightmares. If enzyme deficiency is not addressed, more serious problems can result including obesity, adult onset diabetes and cardiovascular disease. Allergies, gallstones, chronic indigestion and some forms of cancer are all linked to enzyme deficiency. Some authorities believe that *all* disease can be linked to enzyme deficiency. That's a scary thought considering most people are enzyme-deficient to one degree or another.

See if Susan's symptoms sound more like yours:

Susan had been relatively healthy until recently. Her knee and hip joints are often sore, her fingernails are brittle, and her hair breaks easily and is more gray. A cut on Susan's hand is healing very slowly. She has developed an ulcer that gives her a great deal of pain, and her menstrual cycle has become irregular.

What Susan needs is more minerals. Signs of mineral deficiency also include impotence, stretch marks in the skin and slow hair growth. Persistent mineral deficiency leads to atherosclerosis, prostate problems, ulcers, heart attacks and a higher risk of cancer.

Your symptoms may be different from these examples. Your body may be telling you it needs calcium if you have insomnia, tooth decay, muscle cramps or numbness and tingling in your arms and legs.

Chances are your "friendly flora" has been depleted if you have frequent colds or flu, if your energy levels are low, or if you feel sick when you drink milk or eat other dairy products.

Heeding the Alarms

When the alarms go off telling us we need to replenish vital nutrients, we often take action that only compounds the problem. When the oil light comes on in your car, you wouldn't think to "fix" it by unplugging the light or covering it over with a Band-

Aid. Yet often when it comes to our health, we seem to worry more about the "oil light" than about the fact that our bodies need the "oil." We may turn to over-the-counter drugs, stimulant herbs or sugary junk foods, alcohol, caffeine, nicotine or even illegal drugs for temporary stimulation and what we think is relief. As problems persist, we seek a doctor's advice, again, looking for treatment of the symptoms but not getting to the cause.

Your body requires a constant supply of vitamins, minerals, enzymes and "friendly flora." Procrastinating or yielding to cravings for junk food or temporary stimulation will only make things worse, further depleting the body's nutrient supply. That precious supply is further exhausted by environmental factors such as pollution, and physiological factors, such as stress and lack of sleep.

No wonder your body may be trying to get your attention. How can you continue to function if your nutrient supply is in constant demand, but is never replenished?

As we asked the question, "Do I need replenishment?" we were concerned about a number of issues. We wanted to know if all the nutrients we each need could be obtained from food and if any of the nutritional supplements on the market were beneficial. As we met with leading experts in the area of whole food vitamins, minerals, enzymes and probiotics (or good bacteria), and as we did in-depth research of our own, we found some disturbing answers.

First, supplementation *is* necessary for virtually every individual because of risks that are closely linked to our lifestyle practices. In other words, because of our way of life and our environment, supplementation is essential. We *must* replenish certain nutrients if we are to have health.

However, contrary to what some companies try to make you think, there is a right and a wrong way to go about supplementation. Taking everything in the health food store is not necessary. Companies that carry hundreds of different nutritional products are practicing deception and big-time "overkill" about what is really needed for health.

Only Five "Essential Nutritionals"

There are basically five areas that need to be addressed as a foundation for every individual. In other words, although you may have additional replenishment needs depending on your fitness levels and goals, based on in-depth research we have found that there are basically only five "Essential Nutritionals." Our formulation team determined that a nutrient must be needed by at least 90 percent of the population to be included in this list of Essential Nutritionals.

1. First, We Need to Replenish Enzymes

First, virtually every person needs to replenish the essential, life-promoting, highly specialized protein molecules called enzymes. Few of us understand the importance of enzymes; yet, enzymes are vital to every biochemical process in the body. Without enzymes you couldn't breathe, your heart wouldn't beat, you couldn't move your muscles and it would be impossible for you to digest your food. In fact, digestive problems such as constipation, gas, heartburn, bloating, and stomach cramps are often the first signs that you may be deficient in enzymes. Enzyme deficiency leads to headaches, food allergies, premature aging, and some believe that enzyme deficiency may be a precursor for every other disease. And yet every one of us is enzyme-deficient.

How can we make such an absolute claim? What is it that is robbing each of us of something so important? The answer is simple. Digestive enzymes are found naturally in foods, yet they are destroyed at temperatures of 118° F or above. That means most of the current methods of processing and cooking food destroy enzymes. Since virtually every one of us eats cooked and processed foods, every one of us is deficient in enzymes.

Enzymes begin working immediately when we eat raw foods. They help to break that food down and make it available for use in the body. However, when cooked and processed – or in other words, enzyme-deficient – food is consumed, the body must handle the extremely energy-consuming task of digestion by using its own limited enzyme supply. When the body is forced to handle the demands of digestion, the body's enzymes become depleted and chronic digestive problems and other health conditions increase. Statistics show that one in thirteen hospital admissions is tied to a digestive problem. Yet, the initial signs of enzyme deficiency – indigestion (incomplete digestion) – are often treated wrong. Instead of using supplemental digestive enzymes to ensure complete digestion, the signs of enzyme deficiency are often treated with medications such as antacids or acid-blockers which interfere with digestion. This means the symptoms are relieved, but the cause has not been eliminated; and the side effects of these drugs are creating monumental problems.

Enzymes must be replenished for proper digestion, but also, to keep every other bodily process functioning optimally. Without enzymes the body is overtaxed; we fatigue more easily, have more digestive problems, we are sick more often and we age more rapidly. Yet, supplementing enzymes is easy. All you need to do is to take a good pure plant enzyme formula each time you eat cooked and processed food. The Replenishment chapter provides additional information about enzyme replenishment and shares what the experts recommend that you look for in an enzyme supplement.

2. Friendly Flora Need to Be Replenished

Next, another need for supplementation stems from the fact that our friendly flora have been depleted. "Friendly flora" refers to the beneficial bacteria strains that live in our intestines. Health depends on these friendly flora strains which are often called "probiotics" meaning, "favoring life."

These vital microorganisms decrease blood fat and cholesterol levels, help correct yeast overgrowth, and also promote proper elimination, helping to rid the body of toxins. Friendly bacteria also improve digestion, especially aiding in the digestion of milk and milk products. Without friendly flora, harmful bacteria strains can colonize in the intestine, causing infections and chronic diseases; including serious conditions such as rheumatoid arthritis, colitis, diabetes, meningitis, thyroid disease and bowel cancer.

A campsite analogy illustrates the way friendly flora work. If you were to drive into a campground and all the campsites were taken, you would drive right through and look for another place to camp. The same kind of thing happens when a harmful strain of bacteria enters your system. If the intestine is already flourishing with good bacteria strains, the harmful bacteria must "drive right through." With no place to implant, the harmful bacteria cannot colonize and grow. Thus, probiotic strains of bacteria are a "second immune system," protecting us from harmful strains.

Without helpful bacteria strains, we are unable to fight the infectious diseases that have been rising sharply in recent years. Ten years ago, infectious disease was thought to have been nearly eradicated, but has again become one of the leading causes of death. We are more prone to colds and flus, and we have seen a rise in antibiotic-resistant strains of germs called "super germs."

Just what is it that is depleting our flora and making replenishment of friendly flora necessary? Our supply of good bacteria is destroyed by laxatives, birth control pills, carbonated drinks, alcohol and digestive aids (like Tums, Rolaids, Zantac and Tagamet). Stress also depletes our friendly flora. However, the biggest cause of flora depletion is the over-use of antibiotics. Individuals who think they have not had antibiotics recently, may not be aware that half the antibiotics produced are used for animals. If you eat meat, milk and other animal products, you are likely getting antibiotics too.

To protect ourselves, we must replenish our helpful bacteria. Since friendly bacteria supplements are often incomplete and, therefore, ineffective, refer to the Replenishment chapter to learn about what to look for in a bacteria supplement.

3. Environmental Effects Create the Need For an Antioxidant

A third reason we need replenishment is because of our current environment. Environmental toxins, stress, electronic devices, sunlight and over-exercise create highly reactive molecules called "free radicals." Simply put, free radicals are oxygen molecules that are missing an electron. In the body, these unpaired electrons look for another electron to latch onto. To pick up the one electron they need, free radicals bombard healthy cells, robbing one electron from paired molecules, and, thus, creating additional free radicals. This process is called oxidation.

Experts estimate that our cells take over 10,000 "hits" from free radicals daily. This weakens the cell membrane and leaves us prone to disease. A healthy cell is round, with a well-defined, thick cell membrane. A cell that has been bombarded with free radicals is misshapen, and the cell membrane is weak. Over 85 different diseases, particularly conditions like cancer, arthritis, stroke and Alzheimer's disease, have been linked to free radical damage.[29] To neutralize the deadly effects of free radicals (oxidation), an "antioxidant" is required. In recent years, antioxidants have received much publicity. While that publicity has helped the public to understand the importance of antioxidant supplementation, there is a great deal of misinformation about the proper kind of formula to take. In the Replenishment chapter, you will learn how to identify which kind of antioxidant is best and how much you need to take.

4. A Multi-vitamin Supplement is Necessary

Fourth, the formulation team has determined that at least 90 percent of the population needs a multi-vitamin supplement. Due to modern processing and growing methods, our current food supply is devoid of essential nutrients. For example, cabbage, once high in vitamin C, today has none. Wheat, once as high as 17 percent protein, now contains only 9 percent.[30] Soil depletion, depletion of the ozone layer, and environmental toxins, such as pesticides and smog, rob our food of nutrients.

Gradually, even a minor deficiency in nutrients can cause a wide range of maladies, including hair loss, white spots on nails, oily or dry skin, fatigue, mood swings and joint ache. People who look and feel healthy may still be experiencing subtle effects of a diminished supply of nutrients. Nutrient deficiencies cause us to age prematurely, be mentally sluggish, or suffer with back pain, arthritis, asthma, allergies or other chronic conditions. If we don't have the nutrients we need, we don't heal properly after an accident or surgery. Think about some of the telltale symptoms that you may currently be experiencing.

Chapter Two: Do I Need?

Have you ignored the initial warning signs of nutrient deficiency, thinking they weren't "that bad" or that they would go away? A multi-vitamin supplement is necessary for most individuals today.

While there are many of these products on the market, few are in a form that can be readily used by the body. Whole food vitamins are essential. You can learn more about these important nutrients in the Replenishment chapter.

5: A Mineral Supplement is Necessary

There are some compelling reasons to include a mineral supplement as part of your replenishment program. Infinity[2] has always felt that the major source of minerals should be a healthy diet. However, several factors have influenced the formulation team to include minerals as part of the "Essential Nutritionals".

- The refining process used to make breads and cereals and other grain products removes as much as 75% of the minerals including zinc, chromium and manganese. Most of these minerals are not added back to the food even with the fortification process.

- Depending on age, up to 75 percent of U.S. females ingest less than the RDA of calcium.

- Even though we advocate a diet consisting of whole, fresh and raw foods as a first principle of health, we are aware that most people in our society have very busy and pressure-packed lifestyles making it very difficult to maintain a completely healthy food intake. Only 9% of the American population consumes the recommended 5 servings of fruits and vegetables each day.

- Studies have revealed an alarming decline in the mineral content of commercially grown foods.

Clearly, these results warn us that the foods that we have relied upon for our nutrient minerals are no longer dependable sources. For these very compelling reasons, we are convinced that a complete, high-potency supplemental intake of all the nutrient minerals should be a part of the core nutritional supplementation program.

There are many mineral products available on the market, but few are in a form that can be used by the body. In the Replenishment chapter, you will learn more about the importance of minerals and how to identify which kind of mineral is best and how much you need to take.

Diets High in Fats and Sugars Make Replenishment Imperative

Last, we found that many people face health concerns because fats and sugars are so common in our diets. These dietary abuses cause obesity and lead to other problems, even for people who do not have excess body fat. A diet high in fat can cause undigested fats in the blood stream, which contributes to heart disease and artherosclerosis, the leading causes of death today. Excess sugar results in mood swings, cravings, depression and even diabetic or hypoglycemic tendencies. Many foods have "hidden" fats and sugars, so we often consume more than we should. Statistics show  that an average of 140 pounds of sugar and 58 pounds of fat are eaten by every person in North America annually. Even individuals who now limit their consumption in these areas may have lingering problems because of past eating habits. To combat the health risks created by these habits, our formulation team determined that most people need to replenish lipase and chromium. Many people have been amazed at the results they can achieve by taking a lipase/chromium formulation. To learn more about what such a supplement can do for you, refer to the Replenishment chapter.

Also, in the Replenishment chapter, you will find out how each of these five "Essential Nutritionals"areas affect you, and how you can meet your individual supplement needs. Most importantly, you will discover that by modifying your lifestyle habits as described in this book, your replenishment needs will decrease and you can cut back the number of supplements you need to take.

"Quality Control" Warranted When Selecting Supplements

Along with quantity of supplements, quality must also be addressed. Not all supplements are the same; many on the market have even been shown to be harmful. With input from a council of experts, we have outlined a specific set of criteria that we use in the formulation process. This basic product philosophy includes five standards we consider whenever a formulation is created. These standards can serve as guidelines to help you evaluate any nutritional product.

First, a formulation **must provide cellular delivery**. In other words, it must be formulated in such a way that the nutrients reach the body's cells. Any supplement can be ingested, but many are not in the form that can be fully digested and assimilated by the body. However, research shows that certain "delivery systems" ensure that the nutrients reach the tissue sites where they will be used for regeneration and healing. Rather than looking at how many ingredients are in a product, look at whether those ingredients will actually be delivered.

Second, since the body functions as a whole, every system works in harmony, and no organ works independently of another — a viable **formulation must be wholistic**. Each formulation must contain the full spectrum of ingredients necessary for a synergistic interaction to occur. The harm that can come from isolating an ingredient and not heeding this wholistic aspect can best be illustrated with an example. A few years ago, it became a popular practice for women to take high doses of vitamin B_6 to combat fluid retention and PMS symptoms. Many had good results at first, but that high dose of only one of the B vitamins without the other necessary components led to severe nerve damage and, in a few cases, even death.

Third, a formulation **must obey the laws of nature**. Ingredients should be as natural as possible. Overwhelming evidence demonstrates that trying to "improve" on nature by creating synthetic, man-made ingredients invariably fails. Margarine, for example, was introduced as a supposed improvement over the more natural butter. Yet, studies now prove that margarine contains significant amount of trans-fatty acids, which lead to heart disease, margarine is much less healthy than butter. To be health-promoting, a supplement must contain ingredients in their most natural state.

Fourth, every formulation **must be backed by research**, not just promoted with hype. This means a formulation should include only the highest quality, thoroughly tested ingredients. Often, patents set ingredients apart as those that have demonstrated effectiveness.

Last, each formulation **must be something the body needs**. Today there are many ingredients, such as stimulant herbs or colloidal minerals, that are not required by the body, but are included in a formulation because of marketing trends. To be health-promoting, a formulation shouldn't provide only temporary sensations, but should replenish what is missing from the body.

Replenishment Recap

There is definitely a need for supplementation. Our current lifestyles and the environment we live in make it difficult, if not impossible, to get all the nutrients we need from our foods. We must replenish enzymes to aid in digestion and preserve the body's energy supply. We need to restore our friendly flora as a "second immune system" for our bodies. An antioxidant supplement is necessary to ward off the effects of free radicals and multi-vitamin and multi-mineral supplements are more necessary now than ever before. The lingering effects of over-consumption of sugars and fat must be addressed with a lipase/chromium supplement.

Though replenishment is important, we want to stress again that you can't get optimal health from a bottle. In the Replenishment chapter, there is a handy question and answer form to enable you to determine your individual replenishment needs and to help you identify areas in which you need to make lifestyle changes. To improve your health, look first at your lifestyle practices. Make the necessary changes, and then use supplements only to replenish what's missing. Fill out the questionnaire again in a month to see how the lifestyle changes you make have helped to reduce the number of supplements you need to take.

Generates You

The last two letters of the acronym E.N.E.R.G.Y. stand for "Generates You." In other words, by applying the proper principles of Envision, Nutrition, Exercise and Replenishment outlined in *Complete Physique* you can Generate a healthier You.

The "G" and "Y" signify that this amazing program helps you go beyond the mere absence of sickness and disease to a state of well-being and vitality that you may not even be able to fathom right now. Interestingly, just as an electrical generator requires a switch to turn it on and have it produce the desired results of electrical power, we have found that there is a "switch" that must be turned on in order for individuals to generate optimum levels of health. This last aspect of the program, this "switch," is the part that we enjoy sharing the most; it is the part that many overlook, yet it can often do the most to take people to new heights of health.

A Universal Law

We often state it like this:

> *To achieve optimum health, you must first search out true principles and live them, and then, in order to attain lasting peace and true happiness, you must share those principles with someone else.*

This is a time-proven, universal law. What you share will come back to you tenfold. The Institute for the Advancement of Health conducted a study of over 1700 women who were involved in helping others on a regular basis. The study showed that these women had "relief of actual physical ailments in the wake of helping. Disorders such as headaches, loss of voice, pain due to lupus and multiple sclerosis and depression improved."[31]

Herbert Benson, a Harvard cardiologist, said that helping others releases "natural opiates" which "produce the good feelings that arise during social contact with others."[32]

Dr. David Felten, professor of neurobiology and anatomy at the University of Rochester School of Medicine, said, "people are crying out for someone who cares for them, someone who will sit down and actually listen to them and hear how their condition affects them. ..."[33]

Be "Someone"

Complete Physique is ideal for sharing. In fact, as you make lifestyle improvements, you will find the program almost shares itself. People around you will begin to notice changes and will ask you what you're doing for health. You can be that "someone" Dr. Felten describes who will listen and share this powerful program. As you help others, increased health and heightened well-being will return to you.

One other health benefit can come as a result of switching on the generator and sharing health with others, and that is money! Worry over money has been shown to be a leading cause of stress-related health problems. Regardless of how stable you are physically, you cannot have complete peace of mind and total wellness if you are hampered by constant worry over finances.

Because of these things, we realized just how comprehensive our message of health really is. This program has it all — from the foundation of vision, to the principles of true health, and the opportunity for relief of financial bondage. By drawing from experts in all areas, not just in health, but in the areas of marketing, of mind/body technology and of money management, we have been able to provide a program that truly has the capability to "enhance and enrich the quality of life for millions of people worldwide."

We enjoy and appreciate the opportunity to be a part of this mission, and we encourage you to decide how you can become involved. It might simply be to improve your own health, and that's fine. It might be to share the principles of *Complete Physique* with your family and close friends. Or, it might be to become a member of the team that is dedicated to taking health to the world.

However you choose to proceed, please realize that any step toward health, no matter how small, is a step in the right direction. This section has explained "why" taking a step is so important; read the rest of the book to learn "how." Even if you start out slowly, be consistent, and you will steadily move forward to even greater health and well-being.

Chapter Three
Envision

Chapter Three

Envision

Have you ever heard the old cliché used to describe someone as "the picture of health?" Interestingly, "the picture of health" is more than a cliché, it's a practice that will make the difference between success and failure as you undertake this program of health.

To change your health, you must first change your mind! In other words, you must first create a new mental picture of the healthy person you want to be.

As we start to suffer the effects of an unhealthy lifestyle, it's easy to notice when we don't feel well. We create and reinforce our mental picture of health by saying and thinking things like, "I *always* feel so tired," "I have a headache *every* day," or "I *can't* seem to lose any weight."

In order to change those patterns, we must change the way we envision our health. Well-known author and health center director Dr. Deepak Chopra says, "For every state of consciousness, there is a corresponding state of physiology."[1]

In other words, if our "state of consciousness," — the way we envision ourselves — is a mental picture of being "overweight," "tired," and "out of shape," an actual physiological response will take place, bringing those negative pictures into reality. Our bodies respond to create the things we picture. By applying this same principle in a positive way, we can create health by forming a healthy mental image of how we look and feel.

Mental Images Create Physical Reality

Research into the interplay between mind and body has scientifically proven the power of mental pictures. "Your nervous system cannot tell the difference between an actual experience and one that is vividly imagined,"[2] writes lecturer and plastic surgeon Dr. Maxwell Maltz in his best-selling book, *Psycho-cybernetics*. Studies cited by Dr. Maltz show that any endeavor, whether it's golf, throwing darts, playing the piano or playing chess, can be improved through mental imagery. In one study, players who physically practiced shooting basketball free throws improved 24 percent, while

those who practiced only mentally for the same time period improved almost as much — 23 percent.[3]

In his book, *The Book on Mind Management*, human productivity expert Dr. Dennis R. Deaton writes, "A new mental creation precipitates a new physical or behavioral creation. ... People can make dramatic, stunning changes in short order by simply altering their thoughts."[4] When you have a mental vision of what you want to accomplish in any area, the body can't help but respond. Once you have envisioned a goal, you, too, will be led to the things you need to accomplish that goal.

We have come to understand that the most important thing we can teach people is to envision health and vitality. Even with all the knowledge the world has in nutrition and sports medicine, we can often help people most by teaching them to create a healthy mental image. While an exercise technique or a nutritional plan may be important, the most vital element is vision.

Action Item

To ensure success as you undertake this program of health, first and foremost, create a vision, a clear mental image of the kind of fitness and energy you want. To do so, find a picture that signifies what health "looks like" to you. It may be a photograph of yourself at a time in your life when you felt and looked your best, or perhaps a magazine picture which shows the kind of physique you would like to have. If one picture alone doesn't help you envision health, find a second picture that represents energy or vitality. For example, other people have chosen to use a picture of a sleek, strong animal, a powerful machine or a well-tuned automobile. Select a picture that symbolizes energy for you.

Put these pictures where you will see them often — on your mirror, on your refrigerator, or in your office. From time to time, you may want to move the pictures to a new location or add a written caption to help strengthen the visual image. Remember, you are trying to create a strong mental picture of what health looks like to you.

Don't neglect this assignment. It may seem simple, but it's vital to your success. **Creating a mental picture of fitness and energy is the most important thing you can do as you begin your program for health.**

Here are some other ideas that may help as you envision health:

1. Make your picture of health specific and give yourself a starting "baseline" by evaluating where you are now. There are three kinds of measurements we would encourage you to take at the beginning of your program: Body Fat Percentage, Body Mass Index and Waist-to-Hip Ratio. You will find complete instructions for calculating these measurements in the Appendix. Along with taking measurements, we recommend you also take "before" pictures. Then, put both the pictures

and the measurements away. They shouldn't be used to create negative mental images, but should serve as a motivational starting point and a way to assess how rapidly you are reaching the health you envision.

2. **If you choose to write your goal down**, write more than facts and figures. For example, don't say, "I want to lose 10 pounds," or "I want to add 3 inches of muscle." Instead, write a brief description, or what Dr. Deaton calls a "mental movie script"[5] of your accomplishment. Describe yourself (in vivid color!) stepping into a smaller size of your favorite pair of jeans and having them fit perfectly! In other words, paint a word picture of a specific event that signals your accomplishment, and describe how you will look and feel when you reach your goal.

3. **Hold vision sessions** to reinforce your mental pictures. Take a few minutes each day to sit back, relax and let the picture of yourself in your fittest state come to your mind. A good time to do this is just before you go to bed or especially during your exercise workout. Imagine that you are already the fit, shapely, healthy person you are picturing. Make this vision session as "real" as possible as you think about and enjoy all the sensations of health.

We recommend that you stop reading right now and create your vision of health. Complete the assessment in the Appendix, then find the pictures that will help you visualize success and place them in a prominent place.

Remember, in health, as in every other endeavor you undertake, your vision drives your accomplishment. Philosopher Dr. Henry Emerson Fosdick says, "Hold a picture of yourself long and steadily enough in your mind's eye and you will be drawn toward it. Picture yourself vividly as defeated and that alone will make victory impossible. Picture yourself vividly as winning and that alone will contribute immeasurably to success. Great living starts with a picture, held in your imagination, of what you would like to do or be."[6]

Nutrition

Including Recipes and Menus

Chapter Four

Nutrition

This chapter will help you dispel the fallacies about nutrition and will teach you how to eat nutritiously so you can balance your body and move to greater levels of health. We are constantly bombarded with misinformation about nutrition. Evidence shows that even sources that have been regarded as authorities in this area have not promoted the truth. We are being tugged from one food fad to another by special interest groups, fast food promoters and junk food pushers; and the results are startling.

Nutrition-related diseases account for eight out of ten of the leading causes of death, and 95 percent of the population is deficient in at least one vital nutrient[1]. The only way we can escape the current fiasco and have our health intact is to take responsibility for the way we feed our body.

Taking Control

The *Complete Physique* Nutrition Plan gives you everything you need to take control of this vital aspect of health. In the "Do I Need" chapter you received background information that can supply the education and motivation needed to make some changes. Now, in this chapter, you will receive the tools to easily implement a program of good nutrition. You will understand the basics of good nutrition, learn how to set up your kitchen to promote health, and receive the menus, recipes and shopping guidelines to quickly get started. You will also find suggestions for eating at your favorite fast-food establishments and restaurants without compromising your health.

> *Studies on both normal weight and obese people*
> *who followed low-calorie, nutrient-deficient diets for several weeks*
> *showed a 15 percent to 30 percent drop in their metabolic rates*
> *(in the amount of calories they burn in a day).*

The suggestions are simple to apply and will generally fit easily with the way you currently eat. Other ideas may seem new and different at first, so you may need to make changes one step at a time. However, keep in mind that the *Complete Physique*

Nutrition Plan is the most-health promoting plan you can find and that the closer you get to complying fully with the recommendations, the better you will look and feel. Start out slowly if necessary, and realize that making even small changes will provide you with rich rewards in terms of health and well-being.

The importance of nutrition can't be overstated. As Robert E. Windom, M.D., former U. S. Assistant Secretary of Health, says, "Diseases such as heart disease, stroke, cancer and diabetes remain leading causes of death and disability in the United States. Substantial scientific research over the past few decades indicates that diet can play an important role in prevention of such conditions."[1]

The 1988 Surgeon General's Report stated, "For the two out of three adult Americans who do not smoke and do not drink excessively, one personal choice seems to influence long-term health prospects more than any other: What we eat."[2]

> *Eight out of 10 top causes of death in America*
> *today are directly related to our diet.*

What we eat is a crucial consideration. However, even more importantly, we must be concerned with what we digest. We often tell people, "Not just what we eat, but what we digest determines our health." The principle of proper digestion is at the root of every recommendation we make in this section. The foods and the preparation methods described are those that promote digestion and nutrient delivery.

At the outset, we recommend that the five basics listed below become "laws" in your own personal commitment to health. Use these recommendations as a beginning, implementing one at a time if necessary; then, stick to them faithfully. These recommendations identify the biggest culprits when it comes to disease and ill-health. Don't let your own lack of willpower, your busy schedule, your vacations or anything else get in the way of taking a giant step toward health. Following these suggestions will free you from many health hazards.

The Basics

1. No carbonated beverages.

Instead of carbonated beverages, drink fresh fruit juices and water. Some people think we make this suggestion because the caffeine or the sugar in many carbonated drinks is unhealthy. It's true that caffeine and sugar are detrimental, but even non-caffeinated drinks that are carbonated, including the now popular "sparkling water" drinks, create problems for health. The acid in these drinks interferes with digestion. Perhaps that helps you understand why people who drink "diet" sodas still seem to have trouble losing weight.

2. No white flour products.

Stick with grains as they come from the earth. Select whole grain breads and pasta. whole grain breads and pasta are higher in fiber and other essential nutrients.

3. Cut way back on sugar.

Especially, watch for sugars that appear on labels, "hidden" as such things as "glucose" or "corn syrup." Substitute fructose for other sugars.

4. Eliminate fried foods.

Although fat is necessary in the diet, the fat in fried foods is enzyme-deficient, so it cannot be readily used for energy in the body. Instead of eating fried foods, steam, bake or broil your foods. Better yet, eat them raw.

5. Eat as many raw foods as possible.

Raw foods supply essential vitamins and minerals and contain the enzymes necessary to aid in the digestion of those foods. When you can't eat raw foods, take a plant-based digestive enzyme supplement, and use a whole food vitamin/chelated mineral supplement for ensured nutrition. (See the Replenishment chapter for more details.)

These basics should be your starting point, the "laws" you implement and commit to today. However, *Complete Physique's* Nutrition Plan covers much more than the basics. As we researched the area of nutrition we found that certain principles of nutrition were founded on solid fact. Yet, the nutrition programs we studied often included only one or two of these important principles. Just as we have developed a product philosophy that serves as our guide when formulating supplements, we have pulled together four proven nutritional principles that act as the underlying philosophy of the *Complete Physique* Nutrition Plan. As you use the menus and recipes, you will see that these four principles have been heeded as this plan was created. Also, as you become familiar with these four principles, you will be able to use them as a standard. That is one of the beauties of this plan. *Complete Physique* provides complete guidelines so you have everything you need to begin, but it also teaches the principles behind what we recommend so you won't have to refer to this book every time you plan a meal. You will soon be able to quickly evaluate your food choices and know immediately if they're health-promoting.

Perhaps an easy way to remember the underlying principles of healthy food selection and meal planning is to think in terms of a "square" meal. As you know, a square has four sides and a square meal, or a good food choice, should take into account four elements. We know of no other nutrition plan that regards all four of these important elements.

1. The Eating Right Pyramid

The Eating Right Pyramid is the first principle. On April 13, 1991, an article in the "Washington Post" announced that the U.S. Department of Agriculture was publishing it a long-awaited replacement for the "Basic Four Food Groups." The Basic Four Food Groups charts had been used in schools and community education programs for years to encourage people to eat what were thought to be nutritious meals. The Basic Four plan suggested that food from each of four food groups should make up specific parts of the diet.

The Eating Right Pyramid was released after a decade of research and development. The Pyramid is a visual representation of how to eat foods in a healthy ratio. For example, the bottom of the pyramid, the largest portion, shows grains, illustrating that the majority of food we eat each day (six to 11 servings) should be rice, whole grain breads, pastas and cereals. Pictured next as you go up the pyramid are vegetables, of which three to five servings are recommended daily, and fruits with a recommended two to four servings. Smaller amounts of the foods pictured toward the top — dairy (two to three servings) and protein (two to three servings) — should be eaten. Fats, oils and sweets, pictured at the peak of the pyramid, should be eaten sparingly.

By following the Food Pyramid, our food intake each day should be 60 percent carbohydrates, 20 percent protein and 20 percent fat. Everyone should eat this way. These same ratios are recommended for old and young alike. At the end of the day, we should be able to look at what we have eaten and see that it fits this Food Pyramid principle.

2. Raw Foods

The next consideration in your "square" nutrition plan should be raw foods. Foods in their natural state (raw) contain many nutrients that have been identified. However, there are certain unknown components in raw foods that make them more beneficial than foods that are cooked, processed, or altered from their natural state in any way. We don't yet fully understand all of the things that make raw foods superior, but the benefits of natural foods have been well-documented.

Along with the unknown healthy components that are lost, there are vital nutrients that we do know about that are destroyed when foods are cooked or processed. These nutrients are highly complex protein molecules called enzymes. According to nature's plan, enzymes that occur naturally in foods are supposed to help digest that food and break it down in the body. However, those naturally occurring enzymes are destroyed when foods are cooked or processed.

When we eat cooked or processed foods, the only way those foods can be digested is to draw digestive enzymes from the body's supply. The problem is, the body's ability to produce digestive enzymes is limited and can become depleted. Like an enzyme bank account, we make withdrawals from our enzyme supply when we eat foods that are cooked or processed. Our supply is also depleted by things like carbonated beverages, stress and exercise.

When our supply of digestive enzymes is exhausted, to accomplish the process of digestion the body robs from its reserves of metabolic enzymes that are supposed to be used for other functions of the body. For example, the body must mobilize its immune system to finish the digestive process. The body then doesn't have the enzymes it needs to fight disease and to repair and rejuvenate the body. Enzyme deficiency leads to premature aging, degeneration and disease. With our cooked-food diets, is it any wonder that degenerative diseases are not only increasing, but appearing at earlier stages of life than ever before?

We can make deposits to our enzyme bank account by eating raw, natural foods. Northwestern University's physiological laboratory concluded that enzymes operate according to a process Dr. Edward Howell called the "Law of Adaptive Secretion of Digestive Enzymes." Dozens of university laboratories have since confirmed this law, which states that if some of the food you eat still has the enzymes intact (raw food), the body will not need to produce as many enzymes to digest that food. With raw foods, the body is not overtaxed, and more energy can be used for other processes. Eating raw foods helps maintain health and prevent disease, and even supports the body through the healing process.

Remember:

- **Avoid** foods that are heated to over 118° F.
  (Avoid any cooking, except slight steam.)

- **Avoid** foods that have been pasteurized.

- **Avoid** processed foods (such as white flour).

- **Avoid** carbonated drinks.

- **Eat at least** some raw food with every meal.

3. Fat in Food

The third element that is an important consideration in the *Complete Physique* Nutrition Plan is fat in food. Many programs suggest limiting calories or counting fat grams. Instead, the *Complete Physique* Nutrition Plan recommends that you watch the percentage of fat in your foods. No more than 20 percent of your total caloric intake should be from fat.

Unfortunately, we can't rely on the advertised percentages to paint a true picture. Labels that boast "98 percent fat free" or "50 percent less fat" are misleading. The fat percentages on these labels are based on volume only. For example, if you were to take a bottle of water and put one drop of oil in it, you could say that by volume, that water is 99 percent fat free. Yet, based on calories, it is 100 percent fat.

To determine whether the food you buy is 20 percent fat or less, follow this simple procedure. Look at the label on a particular food. It will show the number of calories per serving and the number of fat grams in each serving. A gram of fat is equal to approximately 10 calories, so to quickly calculate the number of calories from fat, multiply the number of fat grams by 10. Then, divide that number by the total calories per serving, and multiply by 100. If the sum is under 20, that food is acceptable. If not, put it back on the grocery shelf and look for something else.

If you put nothing in your shopping cart that has over 20 percent fat, you can eat at home without having to worry about calculating fat percentages every time.

Below are the numbers listed on the actual label of a "low-fat" meal. See if this dinner would fit the 20 percent fat principle:

97% Fat Free
Frozen Dinner
Nutrition Information

1 Serving = 200 Calories

Carbohydrates . . . . 10 grams

Protein . . . . 13 grams

Fat . . . . 10 grams

Example:
1. **Multiply the total fat grams (10) by 10** to get the total fat calories (100) in one serving.

2. **Divide the result by the total number of calories** in one serving: 100 fat calories divided by 200 total calories equals .5.

3. **Multiply the result by 100** to get the percent of fat. Here, .5 x 100 = 50, meaning 50 percent.

*Half of the calories in this dinner come from fat, so this is **not** a food you would want to purchase.*

What about foods without labels?

Many foods, such as raw fruits, vegetables and meat do not have labels. Here are some guidelines you can use to determine the percentage of fat in those foods.

More information about how to select fats that are the most healthy is given at the end of this chapter. Refer to the Recommended Product/Shopping List, p. 101 and the Recommended Fats Chart, p. 99.

Shopping Guidelines for Foods Without Labels

Recommended Foods:		Use Sparingly:	
Food	**Fat %**	**Food**	**Fat %**
Grains 20%		Beef 60%	
Fruits 10%		Dairy 60-90%	
Vegetables 10%		Pork 80-90%	
Fish 15%		Fats and oils 100%	
Fowl 20-30%			

4. Glycemic Index

The fourth part of your "square" nutrition plan is the Glycemic Index. The *Complete Physique* Nutrition Plan includes this important consideration because extensive research shows that low glycemic foods are most desirable.

Low glycemic foods promote a slow, moderate rise in blood sugar and insulin levels after a meal, which helps keep hunger in check and encourages the body to dissolve body fat by converting it to energy.

In contrast, high glycemic foods cause sudden, unstable swings in blood sugar. The end result is an increase in appetite and irritability, and a greater tendency to convert food calories into body fat.

The *Complete Physique* Nutrition Plan encourages you to include a lot of low and medium glycemic foods in your diet. Also, whenever you eat a high glycemic food, combine it with a food from the low glycemic list in order to help balance the effects. Following this aspect of the plan will help minimize hunger and will reduce the tendency to overeat, thus helping you lose body fat.

Even for those whose main objective is not fat loss, low glycemic foods will help alleviate mood swings and regulate energy levels.

Some points to ponder:

- **Foods that stimulate** insulin surges (high glycemic foods) can cause people to eat 60 percent to 70 percent more calories at the following meal

- **People who consume foods** relatively high in glucose (i.e., white bread, most commercial whole wheat bread, raisins) eat an average of 200 calories more at the next meal than those who eat foods high in fructose (a sugar found in most fruits).

- **Low glycemic foods** can be mixed with modest quantities of high glycemic foods, without causing the blood sugar levels to rise erratically.

Use the list that follows to determine which foods are desirable (low glycemic) and which you should use sparingly (high glycemic) and only in combination with a more desirable food. Remember, this list does not indicate which foods are most nutritious, but which foods raise blood sugar levels.

How-tos

In the remainder of this section, you will find the recipes, menu suggestions, Recommended Product/Shopping List and the suggestions for setting up a *Complete Physique* kitchen and for eating out. These how-tos will allow you to put this plan's four important nutrition principles into practice. However, remember that this plan is designed to help you become self-sufficient. Soon you won't have to constantly refer to this chapter. You will understand the basics of nutrition, and selecting healthy foods will be second nature.

Glycemic Index

Note: This is not a list of "good or "bad" foods as far as nutrients go. Instead, it shows which foods raise blood sugar levels. **Low glycemic** foods are preferred. Eat **medium glycemic** foods anytime, but combine with low glycemic food if you eat more than one or two medium glycemic foods in a meal. Use **high glycemic** foods sparingly, if at all, and only in combination with low glycemic foods.

Low Glycemic				*Medium Glycemic*				*High Glycemic*			
0	10	20	30	40	50	60	70	80	90	100	110	120

Bakery Products

Low Glycemic	Medium Glycemic	High Glycemic
Sponge cake 46	Angel food cake 67	Doughnut, cake-type . . . 76
Apple muffin 44	Flan 65	Waffles 76
	Pound cake 54	
	Croissant 67	
	Crumpet 69	
	Bran muffin 60	
	Blueberry muffin 59	
	Carrot muffin 62	
	Oatmeal muffin mix 69	
	Pastry 59	
	Pizza, cheese 60	

Breads

Low Glycemic	Medium Glycemic	High Glycemic
Barley kernel bread 34	Barley flour bread 66	Bagel, white 72
Oat bran bread 47	Hamburger bun 61	Bread stuffing 74
Pumpernickel 41	Oat kernel bread 65	Kaiser rolls 73
Mixed grain bread 45	Rye kernel bread 50	Melba toast 70
Fruit loaf (wheat bread	Rye flour bread 65	White bread 70
with dried fruit) 47	Wheat bread 69	French baguette 95
	Pita bread, white 57	
	Semolina bread 64	
	Bulgur bread 52	

In general, coarse, European-style whole grains or cracked or sprouted whole wheat breads are low glycemic. 100 percent stone ground whole wheat breads are medium. Avoid most commercial breads, both white and wheat, as well as white English muffins and white bagels.

Cereal Grains

Low Glycemic	Medium Glycemic	High Glycemic
Barley 25	Buckwheat 54	Millet 71
Bulgur 48	Maize 55	Instant rice 91
Parboiled rice 47	Taco Shells 68	Tapioca *boiled with milk* . . 81
Rye 34	White rice 56	
Wheat 41	Brown rice 55	
	Wheat, quick-cooking . . . 54	

Again, whole grains are best. Avoid instant and "quick" grains.

Low Glycemic				Medium Glycemic				High Glycemic			
0	10	20	30	40	50	60	70	80	90	100	110	120

Breakfast Cereals

Low Glycemic	Medium Glycemic	High Glycemic
All-Bran 42	Bran Chex 58	Cheerios 74
Rice Bran. 19	Cream of Wheat. 66	Coco Puffs 77
	Grape-Nuts 67	Corn Chex 83
	Life 66	Corn Flakes. 84
	Muesli 56	Cream of Wheat 74
	Nutri-grain 66	Crispix 87
	Oat Bran. 55	Golden Grahams 71
	Porridge 61	Grape-Nuts Flakes 80
	Shredded Wheat 69	Puffed Wheat. 74
	Special K 54	Rice Chex 89
	Rice Krispies 82	Total. 76

In general, coarse whole grain cereals and compact noodle-like high bran cereals (e.g. All-Bran, Fiber One) are low glycemic. For oatmeal porridges, coarse grain is low glycemic; medium/fine grain ("5 minute" variety) is medium; instant or "quick" oats are high glycemic. Avoid flaked and puffed cereals.

Cookies

Low Glycemic	Medium Glycemic	High Glycemic
—————————	Arrowroot 66	Graham Wafers 74
	Oatmeal 55	Vanilla Wafers 77
	Shortbread 64	

Crackers

Low Glycemic	Medium Glycemic	High Glycemic
—————————	Breton wheat crackers . . 67	Puffed Crispbread. 81
	High-fiber rye crispbread . . 65	Rice cakes 82
	Stoned Wheat Thins 67	Water crackers. 72

Whole grain crackers fall into the medium category. Puffed crackers and most commercial white-flour crackers are high on the glycemic index.

Dairy Foods

Low Glycemic	Medium Glycemic	High Glycemic
Milk, whole 27	—————————	Tofu frozen dessert. . . 115
Milk, skim 32		
Chocolate milk 34		
Yogurt (artificial sweetener). 29		

Most milk products are low glycemic, but beware of ice cream, ice milk and yogurt which are sweetened with sugar and fall into the high glycemic category.

Low Glycemic				Medium Glycemic			High Glycemic			
0	10	20	30	40	50	60	70	80	90	100	110	120

Fruit and Fruit Products

Low Glycemic	Medium Glycemic	High Glycemic
Apple 36	Apricots, canned 64	Watermelon 72
Apple juice 41	Banana 53	Pineapple 66
Apricots, dried 31	Fruit cocktail, canned . . . 55	Raisins 64
Cherries 22	Kiwi fruit 52	
Grapefruit 25	Mango 55	
Grapefruit juice 48	Orange juice 57	
Grapes 43	Papaya 58	
Orange 43		
Peach 28		
Pear 36		
Plum 24		

Most fruit and natural fruit juices are low glycemic. However, fruit juices sweetened with sugar fall into the high category.

Legumes

Low Glycemic	Medium Glycemic	High Glycemic
Baked beans 48		Broad beans 79
Beans, dried 29		
Black-eyed beans 42		
Butter beans 31		
Chickpeas 33		
Kidney beans 27		
Navy beans 38		
Lentils 29		
Lima beans 32		
Pinto beans 39		
Split peas 32		

Pasta

Low Glycemic	Medium Glycemic	High Glycemic
Capellini 45	Macaroni and Cheese . . . 64	Rice pasta, brown 92
Fettuccini, egg-enriched . . 32	Tortellini (cheese) 50	
Linguine 46		
Macaroni 45		
Ravioli, meat-filled 39		
White spaghetti 41		
Whole-meal 37		
Vermicelli 35		

Almost all pasta is low glycemic. Watch what is added to the pasta, like cheese and sauce.

Low Glycemic					Medium Glycemic				High Glycemic			
0	10	20	30	40	50	60	70	80	90	100	110	120

Snack Foods and Confectionary

Low Glycemic	Medium Glycemic	High Glycemic
Chocolate 49	Mars Bar. 68	Jelly beans 80
Peanuts. 14	Muesli Bars. 61	Life Savers 70
	Popcorn 55	Corn chips. 73
	Potato chips 54	

Soups

Low Glycemic	Medium Glycemic
Lentil, canned 44	Black bean 64
Tomato 38	Green pea, canned. 66
	Split pea. 60

*Low-fat soups such as Health Valley or Campbell's Healthy Request soups are low glycemic. Most commercial soups contain substantial fat, starch and salt, putting them in the medium category. Instant soups such as "Cup-of-Soup" usually contain corn syrup and are high glycemic.

Sugars

Low Glycemic	Medium Glycemic	High Glycemic
Fructose 23	Sucrose 65	Honey. 73
Lactose. 46		Glucose 97

Vegetables

Low Glycemic	Medium Glycemic	High Glycemic
Peas, dried 22	Sweet corn 55	Pumpkin 75
Green peas 48	Beet root 64	Carrots 71
	New potato 62	Parsnips 97
	White potato 56	Instant potatoes. 83
	Sweet potato. 54	Baked potato. 85
	Yam 51	French fries 75

*Almost all vegetables are low glycemic, but there are a few exceptions, like squash and carrots. The way a food is prepared contributes to its glycemic index rating. For example, a baked potato is high glycemic, while a boiled potato falls into the medium category.

Meat

*On the low side: shellfish, "white" fish (cod, flounder, trout, tuna in water); venison; chicken and turkey (white meat). In the middle: higher fat fish (salmon, herring); lean cuts of beef, pork and veal. High glycemic: most cuts of beef, pork and lamb; hot dogs, luncheon meat.

Foster-Powell K, Miller JB. International Tables of Glycemic Index. Am J Clin Nutr 1995;62:871S-93S.
Podell, R., The G-Index Diet, New York: Warner Books, 1993.

Menu Suggestions

Below are some ideas for healthy meals. Listed here are only a few of the many options available. From the options shown below, you can see how to use the recipes and shopping suggestions to mix and match items in order to create meals that are healthy and delicious!

Breakfast Options

Option 1
- Protein Pancakes p. 60 or French toast made with egg whites
- Fructose syrup p. 60
- 1/2 banana, orange wedges, or fresh fruit juice
- Raw milk

Option 2
- Egg White Omelet p. 61 or Scrambled Eggs p. 61
- Whole grain toast and "Easy Spread" p. 84

Option 3
- Raw Cereal Blend p. 62
- Raw milk
- Choice of fruit (strawberries, banana, orange wedges, etc.)

Option 4
- Scrambled Eggs p. 61 rolled in Cheese Crisp p. 65
- Salsa p. 87
- Raw milk or fresh juice

Lunch Options

Option 1
- Basic Sandwich p. 73
- Piece of fruit
- Side salad
- Raw milk or Lemonade p. 90

Option 2
- Grilled Chicken and Rice Salad p. 75 or Basic Salad p. 74
- Whole wheat roll or bagel
- Easy Spread p. 84

Option 3
- Cheese Crisp with Vegetables p. 65
- Salsa p. 87
- Sliced avocado
- Side salad
- Raw milk

See also:
Sack Lunch Options
Fast Food Options

Dinner Options

Option 1
- "Pan Cooked Chicken" p. 71
- Perfect Rice p. 86 or Rotini p. 79
- Basic side salad with dressing p. 74
- Raw milk, fresh juice or lemonade p. 90

Option 2
- Beans and Rice p. 79
- Side salad
- Dressing p. 88 or 89
- Steamed Vegetable Platter p. 83

Option 3
- Green Chili p. 70 rolled in Soft Cheese Crisp p. 65
- Basic side salad
- Dressing p. 88 or 89

Option 4
- Spaghetti and Meatballs p. 81
- Cornbread p. 85 or Fresh Baked Bread p. 85
- Bottled olives
- Basic side salad with dressing p. 74

Drink Options
See p. 90; try them all!

     ©2000 Infinity², Inc.

Sack Lunch Options

Whole grain bread, muffin, roll (dinner or sub), or bagel
(For children, you may need to start with partial-grain breads as a transition until children acquire a taste for whole grains.)

Add to bread of your choice:

- Tuna
- Vegetables (lettuce-tomato)
- Raw cheese
- Mayonnaise with expeller pressed oil
- Salt, pepper
- Chicken or turkey breast
- peanut butter, jelly
- Easy spread p. 84

Side Dishes:

- Piece of fruit
- Vegetable with dip
- Raisins
- Raw nuts
- Celery with peanut butter see p. 84
- Raw cheese slices with whole wheat crackers

- 100% fruit, fruit leather
- Fresh juice partially frozen in small plastic jars (freeze drinks in small bottles p. 92)
- Olives
- Pickles
- Dried fruit (unsulphered)
- Raw trail mix
- Low-fat chips or chips made with expeller-pressed safflower oil
- Chocolate chips or candy bars made from unrefined sugars and with raw nuts
- E.N.E.R.G.Y. Bars from Infinity²
- Fruit Fat-burner Bars from Infinity²

Note: Use the options listed above and on the previous page as a starting point for creating your own Master Menu. Personalize your Master Menu so it will work for your household. Remember, this is not a list of what you will eat each day. It is a master record of healthy options that your family enjoys. This Master Menu will give you ideas as you plan your meals and shopping lists. Mount your Master Menu inside a cupboard door for ready access. (See steps for setting up a Complete Physique *kitchen p. 95.)*

Snack Options

See p. 92.

Before buying ingredients for any recipe, please refer to the "Recommended Products/Shopping List" on page 101 for guidelines.

Breakfast Recipes

Breakfast Smoothie
A healthful breakfast in a drink! ·
Easily adapted to suit your particular tastes.

1/2 cup raw skim milk; or 1/2 cup nonfat plain or vanilla yogurt (regular or frozen); or 1/2 cup water plus 2 Tbsp. nonfat milk powder

1/2 cup fresh orange juice, pineapple juice or Lemonade (p. 90)

1/2 banana, fresh or frozen

3/4 cup fruit of choice, fresh or frozen

1/2 tsp. fresh lemon or lime juice (optional)

1/2 tsp. pure vanilla (optional)

1/4 tsp. cold-pressed flax seed oil

1 tsp. raw, organic honey or fructose

1 tsp. raw wheat germ (can start with less until used to it)

1 scoop Infinity[2] Definition powder; or 1 scoop Infinity[2] Proteabolic Protein powder; or 1/2 scoop of each (optional)

3 ice cubes (optional)

1/4 tsp. nutmeg (optional)

Dash cinnamon (optional)

Blend all ingredients in blender. **Yield:** 2 servings.

Serve with whole grain toast, bagel or bran muffin.

Per serving:

Calories: 189.5	Protein: 7.4g	Carbohydrates: 35.7g	Fat: 1.9g

Protein Pancakes

This favorite is a great protein source —
a great way to start the morning!

1 **cup** whole wheat
pancake mix (e.g., Hain
brand pancake mix)
1 **scoop** Infinity² Proteabolic
Protein powder
1/4 **cup** uncooked raw oats
1 to 2 **dashes** salt (optional)
1/2 **tsp.** baking powder
1/2 **tsp.** raw wheat germ
1 **tsp.** fructose (optional)

1/4 **tsp.** cinnamon or
allspice (optional)
1/2 **tsp.** flax seed
2 **Tbsp.** finely chopped
pecans (optional)
1/4 **cup** fruit of choice, fresh or
thawed (e.g., blueberries,
sliced bananas, or even
pumpkin)
1¼ **cup** raw skim milk or water

Mix all ingredients except the fruit and the liquid. Add milk or water to desired consistency. Fold in fruit. Cook on pre-heated griddle over medium heat. Serve with "fruit only" jelly or Fructose Syrup (see below). Yield: 3 servings.

Quick version: Simply add one scoop of Infinity²'s Proteabolic Protein powder to dry pancake powder. Mix as directed on the box, using only egg whites and omitting the oil or substituting applesauce.

Serve with fresh fruit, fruit juice or raw milk.

Per serving:

Calories: 343.7	Protein: 23.2g	Carbohydrates: 51.7g	Fat: 4.9g

Fructose Syrup

You'll love the traditional taste of this fructose syrup.

1 **cup** water
2 **cups** fructose

1 to 1¼ **tsp.** natural maple
flavoring

Bring water to a boil. Reduce heat and add fructose. Stir until dissolved. Add maple flavoring and stir. Remove from heat. Syrup will thicken as it cools. Serving size: 1 Tbsp.

Note: Keep syrup refrigerated.

Per serving:

Calories: 39.2	Protein: 0.0g	Carbohydrates: 9.8g	Fat: 0.0g

Egg White Omelet

Just a little more effort yields this elegant breakfast treat.

6 **egg** whites
1 **Tbsp.** raw or skim milk
Dash salt and pepper
1/2 **cup** fresh vegetables of
    choice (e.g., any color
    peppers, green onions,
    zucchini, onions,
    mushrooms or broccoli)
1 **clove** garlic, minced (optional)

1 **Tbsp.** fresh basil or
    1 tsp. dried basil
1/4 **tomato**, sliced thin,
    then chopped
1 **slice** extra lean meat, pre-
    cooked, chopped (optional)
1 **Tbsp.** raw cheese, grated and
    sprinkled with salt and a
    dash of cayenne pepper

Whip egg whites, milk, salt and pepper with fork. Preheat skillet over medium heat; spritz lightly with oil. Add basil, garlic and vegetables. Stir fry for one minute (optional). Remove vegetables from pan and set aside. Wipe pan and spritz with oil again. When the pan is heated, pour egg whites into the pan and prepare the omelet by adding the vegetables, and then adding the tomatoes and meat just before folding. Add cheese and then fold, or, after folding, top omelet with cheese. Yield: 2 servings.

Note: Can use salsa and Yogurt Cheese (p. 87) to flavor eggs or omelet.

Per serving:

Calories: 107.2	Protein: 16.1g	Carbohydrates: 7.1g	Fat: 1.6g

Scrambled Eggs

A healthy version of the traditional favorite.

6 **egg** whites
1 **Tbsp.** raw milk
Salt and pepper to taste
Green chilies to taste

1 **Tbsp.** raw cheese, grated and
    sprinkled with salt and a
    dash of cayenne pepper

Mix all ingredients except the cheese. Scramble the mixture in a skillet which has been lightly spritzed with extra virgin olive oil and heated over medium heat. Sprinkle with raw cheese and remove from heat. Cover pan to melt cheese. Yield: 2 servings.

Note: Make into a sandwich for a special taste treat for lunch or dinner.

Per serving:

Calories: 56.8	Protein: 11.5g	Carbohydrates: 1.4g	Fat: 1.3g

Breakfast Burrito

So easy you can "throw" these together for a satisfying breakfast.

4 **egg** whites

Raw skim milk to taste

Dash salt and pepper

2 **corn** tortillas, or whole wheat chapati or tortillas

Green chilies

Ketchup or picante sauce (optional)

1½ **tsp.** grated raw cheese

Scramble the egg whites to liking. Warm tortillas in toaster or pan until warm enough to fold. Spread scrambled egg whites on tortilla, and roll like a jelly roll. Top with cheese; add ketchup or picante sauce. Yield: 2 servings.

Per serving:

Calories: 110.1	Protein: 9.3g	Carbohydrates: 13.6g	Fat: 2.1g

Raw Cereal Blend

This good, low-glycemic breakfast provides sustained energy.

1/4 **cup** prepared cereal from cereal list (p. 63)

1/4 **cup** old fashioned rolled oats*

Raw, organic honey or fructose

1 **tsp.** raw nuts or seeds (e.g., slivered almonds, pumpkin or sunflower seeds)

1 **tsp.** raw wheat germ*

Pinch of flax seeds*

Mix all ingredients together and serve with raw milk. Yield: 1 serving.

*These items may taste different from what you're used to eating.
If so, add only one at a time in lesser amounts to your regular cereal,
until you get used to them.*

Per serving:

Calories: 204.0	Protein: 7.1g	Carbohydrates: 40.8g	Fat: 3.1g

The fructose referred to in Complete Physique *is pure crystalline fructose, not high fructose corn syrup, which is inferior. When using fructose in place of sugar, reduce amount by 1/3 to 1/2. When cooking with fructose, use the same amount of fructose as you would sugar. For recipes that don't require cooking, use 1/3 to 1/2 the recommended amount of sugar.*

Other Breakfast Ideas

For low-fat French toast, remove yolk from eggs, beat egg whites with a few drops of water or milk and a dash of salt, pepper and cinnamon (optional). Dredge bread slices through the egg mixture, then cook on griddle that has been sprayed with cooking spray.

For quick, low-fat pancakes or waffles, prepare whole wheat pancake mix as directed on the package. Add uncooked oats, cracked grains, blueberries, bananas, etc. to increase nutrient density and lower overall fat percentage.

Children enjoy a simple breakfast of whole wheat bread or bagels with their choice of topping, e.g. "Easy Spread" (p.84), raw organic honey, "100% fruit" jelly, raw nut butters, etc. Serve with raw milk. This is also a great snack idea.

As a general rule, if bread has no nuts or seeds in it, you can have approximately 1/4 tsp. butter on a piece of toast to equal 20% total fat.

To make cinnamon toast, mix 5 Tbsp. fructose with 1 Tbsp. cinnamon. Spread toast with "Easy Spread" and sprinkle with cinnamon/fructose mixture.

On cold mornings, enjoy a hot bowl of 3/4 cup cooked cracked wheat or old fashioned oatmeal (no rolled or quick oats), plus 1/2 cup skim milk and 1 piece of whole grain toast with 1 tsp. raw butter and 1 tsp. all-fruit spread.

Buy unsweetened cereals (Recommended cereals listed below.) and have 1/2 cup cereal, plus 1/2 cup skim milk and 1 piece of whole grain toast with 1 tsp. raw butter and 1 tsp all-fruit spread. Add fresh fruits and fructose to sweeten.

Recommended cereals:

Note: Any cereal made with whole grain flour(s) that has 2 grams of fat or less and 5 grams of sugar or less per 100 calories is fine. We suggest you try:

- Barbara's Puffins
- Barbara's Shredded Spoonfuls
- Fiber One
- Fiber Wise
- Grape Nuts
- Shredded Wheat and Bran
- Kashi (not puffed)
- Health Valley Muesli
- Nutri-Grain Nuggets

To make brown sugar, blend 2½ cups fructose, 1 Tbsp. plus 2 tsp. unsulfured molasses and 1 tsp. vanilla on high speed in blender or with mixer until color is consistent.

Main Dishes

Soft Tacos
Kids especially love this Mexican treat.

Corn tortillas
Ground chicken or turkey
Hain brand taco seasoning
Diced tomato
Lettuce, shredded

Fresh salsa
Yogurt Cheese (p. 87, optional)
Choice of: 1 tsp. raw cheese or
    1 tsp. avocado per taco

Preheat a nonstick skillet over medium-high heat. Spritz lightly with cooking spray or a drop of extra virgin olive oil. Place a tortilla in the pan and heat tortilla on both sides until softened. Place two plates on top of each other, with the top plate upside down to form a space between the two plates, to keep the tortillas warm. Brown meat and add seasoning. Assemble tacos. Yield: 1 serving.

Serve with fresh salsa, corn, corn on the cob or fruit salad; and raw milk.

Option for meat: Use steamed, broiled or grilled chicken breast that is shredded and seasoned to taste with your choice of seasonings (e.g., Mrs. Dash brand seasoning salt, lemon juice or lemon pepper, cayenne pepper, salt and pepper, garlic or garlic salt, onions, etc.).

Option for taco shells: Place tortillas on a cookie sheet covered with foil. Sprinkle with cheese and broil for approximately 30 seconds to a minute. Serve immediately.

Per serving:

Calories: 154.2	Protein: 11.7g	Carbohydrates: 13.4g	Fat: 6.2g

Tostadas
Serve with soft tacos for a real feast!

Use ingredients listed for Soft Tacos (see above), but add fresh, or one can heated, fat-free refried beans. To make tostada shells, place tortillas on a cookie sheet. (Use an old cookie sheet, as it may warp.) Spray tortillas with cooking spray, then place in oven on broil. Turning once each minute, cook until crisp but not browned; set aside. Assemble tostadas. Yield: 1 serving.

Serve with Steamed Veggie Platter (p. 83) and raw milk.

Per serving:

Calories: 159.2	Protein: 12.2g	Carbohydrates: 18.3g	Fat: 4.3g

Chicken Colorado Tostadas

This tostada is definitely different, definitely delicious!

1 lb. chicken breast, skinless
and boned
2 Tbsp. soy sauce
1/4 cup water
1 cup red chili sauce
1 cup pinto beans, cooked
1 clove garlic, minced

1/4 tsp. garlic powder
1/8 tsp. oregano
6 corn tortillas, toasted
Shredded lettuce
1 medium tomato, chopped
Yogurt Cheese (p. 87, optional)

Trim fat from chicken, and cut chicken into small pieces. In large, covered skillet, cook chicken in soy sauce and water over medium-low heat for approximately five minutes. Turn chicken pieces and cook an additional three to five minutes or until chicken loses its pink color when pierced at the thickest part. Add red chili sauce, beans, garlic, garlic powder and oregano. Simmer five minutes. Serve on toasted corn tortillas (See p. 64, Tostadas), topped with shredded lettuce, tomato and Yogurt Cheese. Yield: 6 servings.

Serving suggestion: Garnish with whole radishes and green onions.

Per serving:

Calories: 155.6	Protein: 17.9g	Carbohydrates: 19.9g	Fat: 1.6g

Cheese Crisps

Makes a quick and easy meal when you're in a hurry.

Whole wheat or corn tortillas
(Corn have the least
amount of fat.)
Diced vegetables (e.g., mushrooms, zucchini, onions)

1 Tbsp. grated raw cheese
per corn tortilla or 1½
Tbsp. per wheat tortilla
Salsa (p. 87, optional)

Cover cookie sheet with foil and place tortillas on top. Sprinkle with cheese and vegetables. Broil in oven on 450° F for about five minutes. Roll each tortilla and secure it with a toothpick, or leave flat. If vegetables aren't used, broil the cheese crisps for approximately one minute. As a main dish, serve with raw milk, salad, and beans or Perfect Rice (p. 86) As a side dish serve cheese crisps with tostadas or tacos. Yield: 1 serving.

Optional step: Pre-heat skillet over medium-high heat and stir-fry vegetables in a few drops of extra virgin olive oil for approximately one minute before adding them to the cheese crisp.

Per serving:

Calories: 92.0	Protein: 3.6g	Carbohydrates: 12.4g	Fat: 3.0g

Broccoli Quesadilla
A fun and flavorful blend!

2 Tbsp. teriyaki sauce
1 small red onion, finely
    chopped
2 garlic cloves, minced
1/2 tsp. cumin
1/4 tsp. chili powder
1 bunch broccoli, steamed
    and chopped coarsely

1/8 tsp. cinnamon
1 can chopped green chilies
6 whole wheat flour tortillas
1/2 cup grated raw cheese
6 cherry tomatoes, quartered
1 cup Yogurt Cheese (p. 87)
1 cup salsa
1 avocado, peeled and sliced

In a large non-stick skillet, heat 1 tsp. teriyaki sauce. Add onions; sauté for four minutes. Add garlic, cumin, chili powder and cinnamon. Cook for one minute. Add broccoli and green chilies. Sauté until crisp-tender. Place tortillas on a cookie sheet. Top each with 1/8 of the mixture. Add cheese and tomato; bake until cheese melts. Fold each tortilla over and top with yogurt cheese, salsa and avocado. Yield: 6 servings.

Per serving:

Calories: 241.7	Protein: 9.1g	Carbohydrates: 34.0g	Fat: 7.7g

Nutritious Nachos
A perfect snack for large gatherings.

Use ingredients listed for Soft Tacos (p. 64), except use baked, fat-free, corn tortilla chips instead of corn tortillas. Place corn chips on a cookie sheet lined with foil. Sprinkle with cheese and place in oven on broil for approximately two minutes. Add other ingredients on the side as desired. May also serve with fresh or fat-free canned refried beans. Yield: 1 serving.

For an added touch, serve tacos, tostadas or nachos with sliced black or green olives. As olives are high in fat, use very sparingly and only for entertaining or special occasions.

Per serving:

Calories: 86.6	Protein: 3.2g	Carbohydrates: 11.7g	Fat: 3.0g

Begin a mealtime tradition of having a side salad made with some dark greens, a vegetable, a few raw nuts and dressing of your choice. (See p. 88 and 89) Serve this First Course Salad at each lunch and dinner meal. Serving the salad first will enhance each family member's interest in eating this "raw" nutrition.

Chicken Enchiladas

Feed a lot of people with this oh, so good recipe!

1 **package** Lawry's brand
enchilada sauce mix
1 **whole** chicken
1 **can** chopped green chilies,
drained (optional)
1 **small** onion, chopped
(about 1/4 cup)

16 **corn** tortillas
1/2 **cup** raw cheese
Shredded lettuce (optional)
Diced tomatoes (optional)
Salsa (optional)
Plain, nonfat yogurt or Yogurt
Cheese (p. 87, optional)

Preheat oven to 350° F. Make enchilada sauce as directed on the package. Cook cleaned chicken in water. Set chicken aside and freeze broth for another meal. When the chicken is cool, debone, tear into strips and put into a bowl. Add green chilies, onions and 1/2 cup enchilada sauce. Mix thoroughly. Spread 1/2 cup enchilada sauce in bottom of baking dish. To assemble enchiladas, spread about 1/3 cup of chicken mixture along one side of each tortilla. Roll each tortilla in a jelly-roll fashion. Place seam-side down in baking dish with sauce. Repeat until chicken mixture is gone. Pour remaining enchilada sauce over enchiladas. Cover and bake at 350° F for 25 minutes or until hot. Remove from oven and sprinkle with grated cheese. Top with lettuce and tomatoes, and/or salsa; yogurt or Yogurt Cheese. Yield: 8 servings.

Serve with large First Course Salad (See tip p. 66), baked tortilla chips and fresh salsa.

Per serving:

Calories: 203.4	Protein: 17.7g	Carbohydrates: 23.9g	Fat: 4.3g

Most chicken and turkey marketed as "lean" ground chicken/turkey is over 50 percent fat. Make sure to read the label. A healthy alternative is to grind your own. To make ground chicken breast: With kitchen scissors or knife, trim all skin and fat from raw boneless chicken breast. Put one cup water and one pound of chicken in the blender. Turn blender on to medium or "grind" setting for approximately two minutes, or until chicken is ground. Use in any recipe.

Salsa Verde Chicken

A favorite southwest dinner dish.

1 lb. fresh tomatillos (or one
  12 oz. can)
2 tsp. extra virgin olive oil
2 chicken breasts, skinned
  and boned
1 small onion, chopped

1 clove garlic, minced
3 whole green chilies, roasted
  and chopped
1 Tbsp. fresh chopped cilantro
  (Chinese parsley)
1/2 cup apple juice

If using fresh tomatillos, remove husks and boil in water until tender. Puree cooked tomatillos in food processor or blender. Spray a non-stick skillet with cooking spray. Heat pan and sauté chicken. Add onion and garlic, stirring until tender. Add remaining ingredients. Reduce heat; cover and simmer about 15 minutes. Yield: 4 servings of 1/2 breast each.

Serve with salad and steamed vegetables.

Per serving:

Calories: 201.2   Protein: 27.3g   Carbohydrates: 11.7g   Fat: 4.9g

Pacific Chicken

So tasty you'll want to save it for special meals
— so easy, you'll want to make it every day!

1/2 tsp. cold-pressed olive oil
1 lb. skinless, boneless chicken
  breast, cut in thin strips
1 medium green pepper,
  cut in strips
1 medium onion, cut in
  thin strips
2 Tbsp. soy sauce

1 jar (12 oz.) Heinz fat-free
  chicken gravy
Cooked brown rice or cooked
  wheat noodles
1 can (12 oz.) mandarin orange
  segments (optional)
Pineapple tidbits (optional)

Spritz pan with extra virgin olive oil. Grill chicken in skillet; set aside. Spritz pan with oil again if needed. Sauté green peppers and onions until soft. Add chicken, chicken gravy and soy sauce to vegetables. Simmer two minutes. Serve over rice or noodles. Top with orange segments and pineapple. Yield: 6 servings.

Per serving:

Calories: 277.8   Protein: 29.0g   Carbohydrates: 26.9g   Fat: 5.6g

Teriyaki Chicken

A Chinese-food favorite.

2 **chicken** breasts,
    skinned, boned
1/4 **cup** teriyaki sauce
3 **Tbsp.** fructose
1/4 **tsp.** ground ginger

1/4 **tsp.** garlic powder
2 **cups** cabbage
2 **cups** broccoli
Chopped onions (optional)
Chopped bell peppers (optional)

Trim excess fat from chicken. Pound chicken with meat tenderizer until it is 1/8 inch thick. In a one-quart saucepan, combine teriyaki sauce, fructose, ginger and garlic powder. Cook five minutes over medium to low heat, stirring frequently. Transfer mixture to medium-sized bowl. Allow to cool and marinate chicken for approximately ten minutes. Broil chicken for five minutes. Use remaining teriyaki mixture to baste chicken. Cook another three minutes, or until fully cooked. Serve over brown rice or wheat noodles. Yield: 4 servings.

Serve with salad and raw vinegar dressing, steamed broccoli and whole wheat toast strips.

Per serving:

Calories: 170.9	Protein: 27.6g	Carbohydrates: 11.5g	Fat: 1.6g

Chicken and Rice

This traditional favorite will soon be popular at your house, too!

2 **boneless** chicken breasts
1 **small** green pepper, cut in
    small strips
1 **small** onion, chopped (optional)
2 **cups** water
2 **cups** kidney beans (soaked
    overnight in water and
    then cooked)

1 **can** (8 oz.) tomato sauce
1 **can** (14.5 oz.) stewed tomatoes
2-3 **cups** fresh or frozen corn
1 **can** (4 oz.) chopped
    green chilies
1½ **cups** brown rice

Grill chicken in skillet. Add peppers and onions, and cook until tender. Stir in water, beans, tomato sauce and stewed tomatoes. Bring to boil. Reduce heat; cover and simmer five minutes, stirring occasionally. Stir in corn and chilies. Bring to boil. Serve over cooked brown rice or stir chicken mixture into rice. Yield: 8 servings.

Serve with raw vegetables, salad or Fruit Salad (p. 86)

Per serving:

Calories: 425.8	Protein: 29.1g	Carbohydrates: 71.5g	Fat: 2.6g

Green Chili

This favorite is sure to hit the spot!

2-3 lbs. skinless, boneless turkey breast

1 small chopped onion

1-2 cans (7 oz.) diced green chilies

14.5 oz. can Mexican Style stewed tomatoes

2 cloves fresh garlic, minced or pressed plus 2 tsp. salt; or 2½ tsp. garlic salt

Pinch each of oregano, fresh cilantro or cumin (optional)

Salt to taste

Place turkey breast in five-gallon Crock-Pot and cover with water. Cook on high for two to three hours. Pour Crock-Pot contents into colander which has been placed in a cake pan. Set aside broth. Remove good turkey pieces from colander (there may be small bones or pieces of skin to discard) and cut into one-inch cubes or shred back into Crock-Pot. Add remaining ingredients and add back broth. Add enough water to cover ingredients in Crock-Pot and cook on high for two to three more hours. Continue to add water as needed. (If you would rather have Chili cook all day, set Crock-Pot on low.) Add salt to taste. Yield: 6 servings.

Per serving:

Calories: 310.9	Protein: 55.7g	Carbohydrates: 11.9g	Fat: 3.8g

Seasoned Grilled Chicken

Whether for a barbecue or special occasion, this chicken hits the spot!

Chicken breasts, boneless, skinless, thawed and rinsed (one per person)

Butter Buds Sprinkles

Lawry's brand seasoning salt

Garlic salt

Lemon pepper

Preheat grill to medium-high. Arrange chicken side by side on a cookie sheet, bottom side of breast up. Sprinkle all chicken pieces with each seasoning. Place chicken on grill, seasoned side down. Season the other side with each seasoning. Grill for approximately eight minutes. Turn chicken over and cook for approximately five more minutes or until no pink shows when a slit is made in the thickest part of the breast. Yield: 1 serving.

Note: Using a spray bottle, spray chicken with water to keep the chicken from drying out.

Serve with a side salad, Fresh Baked Bread (p. 85) and steamed vegetable of choice.

Per serving:

Calories: 116.2	Protein: 25.9g	Carbohydrates: 0.0g	Fat: 1.4g

Pan-cooked Chicken

With three sauce options, this recipe offers great taste and versatility.

3 **medium** chicken breasts, lightly salted and peppered
Ingredients for sauce of choice:

Sauce Option I:

6 **Tbsp.** fructose	1/2 **cup** water
3 **Tbsp.** lemon juice	1½ **tsp.** oat or whole
6 **Tbsp.** soy sauce	wheat flour

Sauce Option II:

1 **small** onion, sliced thin (optional)	1 **can** apricots in own juice (use juice only for sauce — add apricots at end),
1 **bell pepper**, sliced thin (optional)	or 1 can pineapple chucks in their own juice.
2-3 **Tbsp.** fructose	
3 **Tbsp.** soy sauce	

Sauce Option III:

1/2 **cup** barbecue sauce	1/4 **cup** orange juice
1/4 **cup** water	concentrate or fresh
1 **Tbsp.** raw, organic honey	orange juice

Mix sauce ingredients in a large skillet. Add chicken breast and cover. Cook on medium heat for approximately 15 minutes. Turn chicken at least once. Continue to cook until chicken is done, approximately 20 minutes. (Chicken should no longer be pink in the middle when a slit is made at the thickest part.)
Yield: 3 servings.

Note: Add water to pan as needed. At end of cooking time, remove lid and cook until sauce is desired consistency.

Optional: Brown meat in skillet lightly spritzed with extra virgin olive oil over medium-high heat before adding sauce ingredients.

Serve with Perfect Rice (p. 86) or Rotini (p. 79), Fresh Baked Bread (p. 85), First Course Salad (See tip p. 66) and steamed broccoli drizzled with lemon juice, salt and pepper and a touch of grated raw cheese.

Per serving:

Calories: 236.9	Protein: 39.0g	Carbohydrates: 12.4g	Fat: 2.8g

Herbed-Baked Fish Fillets

A good, light meal.

1 to 1½ lbs. fish fillets	1 tsp. freshly grated ginger
1/2 cup whole wheat flour	1 egg white
1/2 tsp. oregano	1/2 cup plain nonfat
1/2 tsp. garlic powder	yogurt

Combine flour and herbs. Dip fish in egg white, then in flour mixture. Place fish in single layer in baking dish. Spoon yogurt over fish. Bake in preheated 400° F oven for about 15 minutes. (For some extra flavor, add a tablespoon of stoneground or Dijon mustard to the yogurt.) Yield: 4 servings.

Per serving:

Calories: 187.2	Protein: 29.8g	Carbohydrates: 13.2g	Fat: 1.3g

Tender Salsa Fish

Can be chilled for a perfect hot-weather meal.

2 4-oz. fish fillets	1 Tbsp. cilantro
1 cup diced tomato	(Chinese parsley)
1/4 cup chopped onion	2 Tbsp. fresh lemon juice
2 Tbsp. diced green chili	1 Tbsp. chili sauce

Top fish fillet with all ingredients. Bake in oven at 350° F until brown. Serve hot or cold. Yield: 2 servings.

Per serving:

Calories: 115.7	Protein: 21.1g	Carbohydrates: 5.0g	Fat: 1.1g

If grilling, sautéing, etc. on stove top with a non-stick pan, heat pan on medium-high heat until water dances when sprinkled in pan. Instead of oil, use a spray bottle of water. Spray item to be cooked, then spray pan and immediately put item into pan. The steam created will both soften and moisten food. If crispy food is desired, once you've followed the above steps, spray food with a small amount of oil and continue to cook until brown. (See list of Recommended Fats p. 99)

Better Burgers

Especially good for your backyard barbecues or outdoor cooking.

Lean ground chicken or turkey breast (3 oz.)
Whole wheat bun
Your choice of seasonings (e.g., Mrs. Dash brand seasoning salt, celery salt, lemon pepper, Lawry's brand seasoning salt — no MSG.)

Stoneground mustard; Essential Mayo (p. 88); mayonnaise made with expeller pressed oils; or barbecue sauce
Lettuce, tomatoes, avocado, pickles, sprouts (optional)

Grill chicken on barbecue grill or stove top. Season with your choice of seasonings (listed above). Place cooked chicken on bun. Prepare with your choice of condiments. Yield: 1 serving.

Serve with First Course Salad (tip p. 66) or Fruit Salad (p. 86), and vegetables with Veggie Dip (p. 89).

Per serving (without avocado):

Calories: 333.4	Protein: 30.4g	Carbohydrates: 39.2g	Fat: 7.0g

Basic Sandwich

At home or on the road, here's a healthy version of an old brown-bag favorite.

2 pieces whole wheat bread (The coarsest, lowest fat bread you can find, or use a whole grain pita pocket or hoagie roll.)
Stoneground mustard (found in health food stores)
Sliced tomatoes sprinkled with your choice of seasonings (e.g., salt, garlic salt, pepper, Mrs. Dash seasoning salt)

Lettuce or sprouts sprinkled with vinegar, salt, cayenne pepper, or other seasonings.
Choice of sliced vegetables, no limit (e.g., cucumbers, mushrooms, bell peppers, yellow or red onions, watercress)
Choice of 3 oz. lean chicken or turkey breast, sliced, grilled or barbecued; or 1/2 Tuna Salad (p. 74).

Note: If you choose turkey or chicken, you may also choose one of the following: 1/4 avocado; 1 tsp. Essential Mayo (p. 88) or mayonnaise made with expeller-pressed oil; 1 tsp. prepared dressing made with expeller-pressed oil, or 2 Tbsp. grated raw cheese. Add peeled, sliced green chilies for an extra flair.

Compile your choice of sandwich ingredients in the order listed. Yield: 1 serving.

Per serving:

Calories: 277.5	Protein: 26.3g	Carbohydrates: 33.8g	Fat: 3.9g

Basic Salad

Add meat to convert this tasty side dish into a meal!

1 **cup** lettuce (dark green or red)

1/2 **cup** spinach leaves

1 **cup** vegetables (e.g., broccoli, grated carrots, diced tomatoes, chopped celery)

Choice of one: avocado, sliced; 1 Tbsp. raw nuts or seeds (e.g., pumpkin or sunflower seeds, walnuts, pecans, slivered almonds, pine nuts); or 1 Tbsp. grated raw cheese. (Add salt or seasonings directly to the cheese for added flavor.)

1/2 **cup** bean sprouts

1/8 **cup** each of frozen corn and peas, thawed (optional)

Choice of one: 3 oz. sliced chicken or turkey breast, cooled and cut into julienne strips; 3 oz. water-packed tuna, drained; grilled chicken breast, cut into strips; 1/2 cup beans of choice (e.g., kidney, garbanzo); 2 hard-boiled egg whites, chopped; 3 oz. taco meat; or 1 1/2 oz. taco meat and 1/3 cup fat-free refried beans

Layer all ingredients; toss if desired. If you choose to make a taco salad, serve with whole grain pita bread or nonfat, baked tortilla chips. Yield: 1 servings.

Dressing choices: Raw vinegar, fresh lemon juice, or salt and pepper. See also page 88. Serve with Cheese Crisp (p. 65)

Per serving:

Calories: 272.5	Protein: 24.7g	Carbohydrates: 27.9g	Fat: 6.9g

Tuna Salad

This is extremely tasty on a toasted whole wheat bagel.

1 **can** water-packed tuna (the lowest fat you can find)

Few drops of pickle or lemon juice, or 1 tsp. vinegar

Choice of 1/2 cup diced celery, onions, apples, bell peppers, dill pickles

1 **tsp.** Essential Mayo (p. 88); or mayonnaise made with expeller-pressed oil; or 1 tsp. cold-pressed safflower or grape seed oil

Mix all ingredients. Salt and pepper to taste. Yield: 2 servings.

Serve with Rotini (p. 79) or Perfect Rice (p. 86).

Per serving:

Calories: 132.3	Protein: 21.7g	Carbohydrates: 4.4g	Fat: 3.1g

Grilled Chicken and Rice Salad

Offers a tasty meal with an Oriental flair!

2 **grilled** chicken
breasts, chopped
2 **cups** brown rice (cooked with
2 tsp. salt in the water)
3 **carrots**, grated

1/2 **bunch** green onions, diced
1/2 **head** cabbage, shredded
(or use pre-packaged
vegetables)

Dressing ingredients:

3 **Tbsp.** fructose
4 **Tbsp. + 1 tsp.** raw red
wine vinegar
1/2 **tsp.** salt
1/2 **tsp.** pepper

1 **Tbsp.** cold-pressed or extra
virgin olive oil
1 to 3 **Tbsp.** water (Start with
one and add more
as desired.)

Note: This dressing may be used alone or with Yogurt Cheese (p. 87) added to any salad.

Mix salad ingredients together; set aside. Mix dressing ingredients; add to salad. Mix well. Top with raw slivered almonds if desired. Yield: 4 servings.

Serve with toasted whole-grain bagel or roll, fresh peas or vegetable of your choice.

Per serving:

Calories: 307.4	Protein: 18.0g	Carbohydrates: 48.9g	Fat: 4.8g

Warm Chicken and Spinach Salad

Add variety to your menu with this yummy spinach salad.

5 **cups** torn fresh spinach leaves
2 **cups** coarsely chopped tomato
1/4 **cup** chopped parsley
2 **whole** chicken breasts
(skinned, boned and cut
crosswise into 1/2 inch strips)

2 **Tbsp.** teriyaki sauce
1 **cup** sliced fresh mushrooms
1/4 **cup** diagonally sliced
green onions
1 **tsp.** Honey Tarragon
Dressing (p. 89)

On six serving plates, layer spinach, tomato and parsley. Stir-fry chicken in teriyaki sauce until lightly browned, then stir in mushrooms and onions and cook one minute. Arrange chicken on top of salad greens. Drizzle with salad dressing and serve. Yield: 6 servings.

Per serving:

Calories: 107.9	Protein: 19.3g	Carbohydrates: 5.0g	Fat: 1.4g

Potato Toppers

Select your favorite topping to turn a potato into a meal.

Leaving the skin on, cut a potato into fourths and boil or steam it until soft. Or, poke a potato with a fork, wrap it in aluminum foil and bake at 350° F until soft (about 45 minutes to one hour). Choose your favorite topping from the following recipes.

Note: You can use Butter Buds Sprinkles to top any potato.

Mexican Potato *(Yield: 1 serving)*

1 cup Chili Beans (from p. 79 or purchased, 20% fat or less)

1 Tbsp. raw cheese
1 Tbsp. Yogurt Cheese (p. 87)

Per serving:

Calories: 295.5	Protein: 15.2g	Carbohydrates: 55.3g	Fat: 2.1g

Pizza Potato *(Yield: 1 serving)*

3/4 cup spaghetti sauce (20% fat or less)
1 Tbsp. raw cheese

Optional items: 1/2 cup diced chicken breast, cooked, skinned and boned; mushrooms; olives; onions; green pepper; etc.

Per serving:

Calories: 212.1	Protein: 7.7g	Carbohydrates: 42.9g	Fat: 1.3g

Teriyaki Potato *(Yield: 1 serving)*

1/4 cup sliced onion
1/4 cup sliced green pepper
1/4 cup sliced mushrooms
1/2 cup broccoli, small pieces

1/2 cup diced chicken breast, cooked, skinned and boned (optional)
Cornstarch

Sauté all vegetables in teriyaki sauce. Add 1/2 cup chicken broth. When vegetables are crisp-tender, remove from pan. Add enough cornstarch to remaining liquid to slightly thicken the mixture.

Per serving:

Calories: 223.1	Protein: 25.0g	Carbohydrates: 26.5g	Fat: 1.9g

Vegetable Potato *(Yield: 1 serving)*

1 cup steamed vegetables (your choice)

1 Tbsp. Yogurt Cheese (p. 87)

Per serving:

Calories: 210.3	Protein: 6.2g	Carbohydrates: 38.5g	Fat: 3.5g

Potato Toppers — continued

Enchilada Potato (Yield: 4 servings)

1 **can** (14.5 oz.) red chili sauce
1 **can** (14.5 oz.) enchilada sauce
1 **can** (4 oz.) diced green chilies
1 **clove** garlic, minced
1 **tsp.** raw cheese

1 **green onion**, chopped
1 **Tbsp.** Yogurt Cheese (p. 87)
1 **cup** cooked, chopped spinach
    (optional) Squeeze out
    excess water.

Combine first four items; simmer for about 20 minutes. Top potato with sauce, spinach, cheese, onion and Yogurt Cheese. Yield: 4 servings.

Per serving:

| Calories: 222.1 | Protein: 6.4g | Carbohydrates: 29.8g | Fat: 9.9g |

Homemade Chicken Noodle Soup

This family favorite makes a good Sunday evening meal,
especially for those cold winter nights!

1 **whole** chicken
1 **pkg.** whole wheat noodles
3 **to 4 stalks** cut celery (opt.)
2 **to 3 cups** water

Seasonings (e.g., garlic salt,
Lawry's brand seasoning salt,
lemon pepper, Mrs. Dash
seasoning salt, celery salt)

Boil chicken in enough water to completely cover the chicken. Remove chicken and place broth in the freezer or in the refrigerator to cool. Debone chicken. When broth is cool, skim off the white part (the fat) from the top. Add seasonings, water and noodles. When noodles are done, add chicken. Simmer to mix flavor. Yield: 2 servings.

Serve with First Course Salad (See tip on p. 66) and Fresh Baked Bread (p. 85).

Per serving:

| Calories: 204.6 | Protein: 22.6g | Carbohydrates: 21.6g | Fat: 3.1g |

Soup tips
- *For a quick, healthy soup, heat one can New England Clam Chowder until boiling, stirring continuously. Add one can raw skim milk and leave on heat just long enough to heat to desired temperature.*
- *To remove fat from canned soup, open can without shaking. The fat will be at the top of the soup. Run the back of a stainless steel spoon over the fat. The fat will stick to the spoon. Wipe the fat onto a paper towel and repeat until all fat is removed.*

7-Bean Soup

Let this delicious soup cook while you're away for the day!
Can be easily prepared for a family or community gathering.

7 **cups** water
1 **bag** (16-oz.) of 7-bean Mix,
    or your favorite mixture
    of dry beans
1 **tsp.** chili powder
1 **8-oz. can** tomato sauce
Salt to taste

The following items, chopped:
  1 **stalk** celery
  2 carrots
  1 **clove** garlic
  1 onion
  1 bell pepper

Seasonings to taste (garlic salt, Mrs. Dash seasoning salt, lemon pepper, celery salt).

Soak beans in water overnight. Combine all ingredients. Cook in slow cook Crock-Pot for seven hours. Yield: 4 servings.

Serve with First Course Salad (See tip on p. 66) and Fresh Baked Bread (p. 85).

Per serving:

Calories: 245.5	Protein: 14.2g	Carbohydrates: 44.7g	Fat: 1.1g

Chicken and Escarole Soup

This soup hits the spot any time of the year!

4 **8-oz.** chicken breasts, skinned
    and boned
1½ **quarts** water
4 **packs** instant chicken broth
    and seasoning mix
2 **cups** diced carrots
1 **cup** diced celery

1/2 **cup** chopped onion
4 **oz.** uncooked noodles
  (any type, wheat
  or spinach)
3 **cups** chopped escarole
1 **Tbsp.** chopped fresh parsley
Dash of pepper

In 4-quart saucepan, combine chicken, water and broth mix. Bring to a boil. Reduce heat to low; cover and let simmer for 20 minutes. Using a slotted spoon, remove chicken from liquid; dice and set aside. Add carrots, celery and onion to saucepan. Add remaining ingredients, including chicken, and cook until noodles are tender (eight to ten minutes). Yield: 4 servings.

Variation: Substitute one cup hot, cooked long-grain rice for the noodles. Do not cook rice with remaining ingredients. Cook escarole mixture until hot (eight to ten minutes); add rice and stir to combine. Serve immediately.

Per serving:

Calories: 269.5	Protein: 41.7g	Carbohydrates: 16.5g	Fat: 3.4g

Chili Beans

An easy-fix chili your whole family will love.

1 **lb.** ground chicken or turkey
1 **pkg.** Hain brand chili mix
1 **can** (15 oz.) kidney beans

1 **can** (14.5 oz.) stewed tomatoes
1/4 **tsp.** fructose (optional)

Brown ground meat. Add chili mix, beans, tomatoes and fructose. Stir and heat. Yield: 6 servings.

Per serving:

Calories: 211.8	Protein: 25.8g	Carbohydrates: 10.5g	Fat: 7.1g

Beans and Rice

House special.

1 **tsp.** extra virgin olive oil
1 **cup** chopped onion
2/3 **cup** chopped green
    bell pepper
2 **to** 3 **large** garlic
    cloves, minced

1 **can** (15.5 oz.) red or black
    beans, rinsed and drained
1 **bay leaf**
4 **cups** cooked brown rice

Sauté onion, green pepper and garlic in oil until crisp-tender. Stir in beans and bay leaf. Simmer ten minutes. Remove bay leaf. Yield: 5 servings.

Serve over rice, or serve with a large salad, olives and Cornbread (p. 85).

Per serving:

Calories: 266.7	Protein: 7.0g	Carbohydrates: 54.9g	Fat: 1.6g

Rotini

Try this for an easy, scrumptious side dish.

6 **oz.** vegetable rotini or
    bow tie pasta, or any
    whole grain noodles
1 **tsp.** extra virgin olive oil

2 **tsp.** butter or Easy
    Spread (p. 84)
1/4 **tsp.** salt (to taste)
1/8 **tsp.** pepper

Cook noodles according to package directions until soft. Drain well. Return to pan, and add remaining ingredients. Yield: 1 serving.

Per serving:

Calories: 347.2	Protein: 8.2g	Carbohydrates: 48.4g	Fat: 13.2g

Barbecue Meatballs

Sweet and saucy — kids love these meatballs!

1/4 lb.(4 oz.) extra-lean ground turkey or chicken breast

1½ cups old fashioned oats, uncooked (or 1 cup cooked brown rice)

3 egg whites

2 Tbsp. finely diced green pepper

1/8 onion, finely diced

1/2 cup favorite barbecue sauce (See Spaghetti and Meatball recipe, p. 81.)

Mix all ingredients together, except barbecue sauce. Make mixture into round, Tbsp.-sized balls, and place them in a frying pan sprayed with nonstick cooking spray. Cook on medium heat for five to seven minutes. Turn balls over and pour barbecue sauce on top. Reduce heat to low and simmer for approximately 15 minutes. Makes 20 to 25 Tbsp.-sized meatballs. Yield: 2 servings.

Serve with Perfect Rice (p. 86) or Rotini (p. 79) and First Course Salad (See tip p. 66).

Per serving:

Calories: 282.0	Protein: 25.4g	Carbohydrates: 28.4g	Fat: 6.5g

Spaghetti

An all-time favorite you'll want to make again and again.

1/2 lb. chicken (boneless, skinless and cut into thin strips), ground turkey or meatballs

Healthy Choice brand nonfat spaghetti sauce*

Steamed vegetables (e.g., broccoli, green peppers, onions, mushrooms, zucchini, squash, cabbage).

Cook chicken, ground turkey patty or meatballs (See recipe for Meatballs, p. 81). Add meat and vegetables to sauce; simmer until hot. Serve over brown rice or whole wheat noodles.

*Any sauce with less than 2 grams of fat per 100 calories is okay. Serve with First Course Salad (See tip p. 66), Fresh Baked Bread (p. 85) and Steamed Veggie Platter (p. 83).

Per serving:

Calories: 345.7	Protein: 32.2g	Carbohydrates: 44.1g	Fat: 2.8g

Spaghetti and Meatballs

Use the same ingredients listed for Barbecue Meatballs (p. 80), except, instead of barbecue sauce, use 1/4 tsp. garlic powder, 1/4 tsp. oregano and 1/3 cup tomato sauce. Cook ingredients together in favorite spaghetti sauce. Serve over whole wheat spaghetti noodles. Yield: 2 servings.

Serve with large First Course Salad (See tip p. 66) and Fresh Baked Bread (p. 85).

Per serving:

Calories: 270.8   Protein: 25.4g   Carbohydrates: 27.3g   Fat: 6.1g

Creamy Chicken Fettuccine

So creamy it's hard to believe it's healthy!

16 oz. whole wheat or spinach fettuccine	**3 tsp.** extra virgin olive oil
1 large garlic clove and 1/2 tsp. sea salt, or, 1/4 tsp. salt and 1/4 tsp. garlic salt	**2 tsp.** whole wheat or oat flour (p. 84)
2 chicken breasts, skinned, boned and diced	**1 cup** skim milk
	1/4 tsp. black pepper
	Salt to taste
	1 Tbsp. raw cheese

Cook fettuccine according to package directions. In a skillet, combine garlic or garlic salt, one teaspoon of the oil, and the chicken. Stir fry until chicken is no longer pink when pierced at the thickest part (about five to eight minutes). Remove chicken from pan and keep warm. Add remaining two teaspoons of oil to skillet and sprinkle flour over mixture. Stir well. Gradually stir in skim milk; bring to a boil, stirring occasionally. Reduce heat to medium; cook one to two minutes, stirring occasionally until mixture thickens slightly. Return chicken to skillet. Add salt and pepper. Drain fettuccine, and add it to the skillet, along with raw cheese. Toss to mix well. Yield: 6 servings.

Serve with spinach salad, whole grain toast and fresh fruit salad for dessert.

Per serving:

Calories: 397.7   Protein: 28.7g   Carbohydrates: 58.5g   Fat: 4.3g

Always keep a jar of fresh lemon juice in the refrigerator as it is an ingredient that appears in many recipes. May also freeze lemon juice in an ice cube tray and defrost as needed.

Italian-Style Kidney Bean Salad

Makes a great main dish salad.

1 can (15.5 oz.) kidney beans, drained and rinsed
1/3 to 1/2 cups nonfat Italian dressing (or Basic Vinegarette, p. 88)

2 medium zucchini, chopped
1 clove garlic, minced
4 oz. (1 cup) raw cheese, cubed
1 cup chopped tomato
Lettuce

Combine first four ingredients. Chill. Serve with tomato and cheese over lettuce. Yields: 4 servings.

Per serving:

| Calories: 159.0 | Protein: 11.5g | Carbohydrates: 14.8g | Fat: 2.5g |

Baked Ziti with Mozzarella

You'll love this luscious dish.

1 can (1 lb.) tomatoes with juice
1 Tbsp. defatted chicken broth
1 medium yellow onion, chopped fine
1 can (8 oz.) tomato sauce
3 cloves of garlic, minced

1/2 tsp. oregano
1 tsp. basil
1/8 tsp. pepper
8 oz. rigatoni or ziti
1 cup grated raw cheese (4 oz.)

Preheat oven to 375° F. In a blender or food processor, puree the tomatoes for 10 to 15 seconds. Set aside. Heat the chicken broth in a heavy 10-inch skillet over moderate heat for one minute. Add onion and cook uncovered until soft (about five minutes). Add the tomatoes, tomato sauce, garlic, oregano, basil and pepper. Bring mixture to a boil; reduce heat to low, and simmer uncovered for ten minutes, stirring often (until sauce has slightly thickened). Cook the ziti according to package directions, omitting the salt. Rinse with cold water; drain well, and place in an ungreased, shallow 1½-quart casserole dish. Cover with the sauce. Bake uncovered for 25 minutes or until bubbly. Sprinkle with cheese and cover with foil. Let stand covered for five minutes before serving. Yield: 4 servings.

Per serving:

| Calories: 321.6 | Protein: 16.4g | Carbohydrates: 50.6g | Fat: 6.0g |

Have a decorative bowl of your family's favorite raw nuts on the table with each meal. Leave the bowl on the counter at all times to encourage your family to eat nuts for a healthy snack. (This is a good way to get everyone in the family used to the idea of eating more raw foods.) A second decorative bowl filled with pure plant enzyme capsules and placed on the table or counter at all times will remind family members to take enzymes with each meal.

Mini Fiesta Pizzas

Fun for Friday night.

3 **whole-grain** bagels (sliced in half) or 4 whole-grain pitas
1 **small** jar pizza sauce
1 **tsp.** dried oregano (optional)
1 **Tbsp.** raw cheese per bagel or pita

Toppings: diced olives, onions, green peppers, mushrooms, pineapple, corn or Mexicorn (Fresh corn cut from the cob is very good)

Preheat oven to 450°F. Line cookie sheet with aluminum foil. Place bagels or pita bread side by side on foil. Spread pizza sauce on top; sprinkle with oregano and cheese. Add toppings of your choice. Place in oven on middle rack for approximately three minutes or until cheese is slightly melted. Yield: 5 servings.

Serve with a large salad or vegetable sticks and Veggie Dip (p. 89).

Note: When eating corn, always chew it thoroughly.

Per serving:

Calories: 206.9	Protein: 10.8g	Carbohydrates: 33.1g	Fat: 4.0g

Steamed Veggie Platter

Your choice of vegetables makes this a versatile side dish.

2 **medium** white potatoes;
1/2 lb. broccoli, cut up; and
1 large sweet potato, cubed
or 3 medium carrots, sliced,
and 15 fresh string beans

Salt and pepper to taste
8 **Tbsp.** grated raw cheese

Steam all vegetables until they can be pierced easily with fork. Keep vegetables warm in the steamer while you prepare the veggie platter. Remove 1/4 of the vegetables and place them on a medium plate. Sprinkle with salt and pepper to taste. Add 1 Tbsp. of the cheese. Cover with a paper plate until cheese is melted. Repeat with another 1/4 of the vegetables, layering until all vegetables are used. Yield: 4 servings.

Note: Any of your favorite vegetables may be used in this recipe.

Per serving:

Calories: 132.0	Protein: 6.7g	Carbohydrates: 21.0g	Fat: 1.35g

Tasty Extras

Oat Flour

Make your own flour to use in all your recipes! Great for thickening sauces.

1 cup rolled oats (health food store variety)

Blend oats in blender on high speed for approximately one to two minutes to make a fine powder. Store in zip-lock bag in refrigerator. Yield: 12 servings.

Per serving:

Calories: 25.9	Protein: 1.1g	Carbohydrates: 4.5g	Fat: 0.4g

Easy Spread

Healthiest "butter" spread there is!

1/2 cup raw butter or butter, softened
3/8 tsp. salt

1/2 cup your choice of cold-pressed, unrefined oils.

Mix all ingredients together until smooth. This makes a spread that is much softer, right from the fridge, than butter. It also makes whole grain breads more palatable because it penetrates into the breads, softening them. (This is also true of the peanut butter version listed below.) Yield: 40 servings (1 tsp. per serving).

Peanut butter version: Use approx. 1 jar (18 oz.) peanut butter in place of butter. May also add 1/2 cup raw almond butter to this mixture.

Per serving:

Calories: 36.0	Protein: 0.0g	Carbohydrates: 0.0g	Fat: 4.0g

Note: You may want to have a separate container of Easy Spread made with almost all oil and very little butter to use when the taste will be covered by honey, jelly, etc. The butter is for taste and texture for spreading only.

- *Use applesauce or mashed bananas in place of oil/butter.*
- *Reduce fat in recipes by using one egg white, or one egg white and 1 Tbsp. mashed bananas in place of one whole egg.*

Fresh Baked Bread

Great as a sweet snack or Italian food side dish.

Whole grain bread slices or sliced bagels
1/4 tsp. Easy Spread (p. 84) per slice of bread
Raw organic honey or garlic salt

Preheat oven to broil. Line a cookie sheet with aluminum foil and arrange bread slices side by side on foil. Broil approximately 30 seconds on each side. Spread Easy Spread on each slice of bread. Add honey or sprinkle with garlic salt. Yield: 1 serving.

Note: You can also try cinnamon and fructose; or peanut butter and jelly or honey.

Per serving:

| Calories: 119.2 | Protein: 4.1g | Carbohydrates: 19.4g | Fat: 2.8g |

Cornbread

A great side dish to serve with chili or soup.

1/8 cup expeller-pressed oil
2/3 cup fructose
2 egg whites
1 cup raw skim milk
1 Tbsp. vinegar

1/2 tsp. baking soda
1 cup coarse yellow cornmeal
1 cup whole wheat flour
1/2 tsp. salt

Preheat oven to 375°F. In medium bowl, mix oil and fructose. Add egg whites; beat until well-blended. Set aside. In measuring cup, mix vinegar and milk. Add soda; stir. Combine vinegar and oil mixtures; stir. Add cornmeal, flour and salt; mix only until blended. Pour batter into a lightly greased or sprayed 8-inch square or small, round baking pan. Bake for approximately 15 minutes. Do not overcook. Serve with Easy Spread if desired (p. 84) and raw organic honey. Yield: 8 servings.

Per serving:

| Calories: 213.2 | Protein: 5.4g | Carbohydrates: 38.9g | Fat: 4.0g |

When ordering salad at a restaurant, ask for avocado, vinegar and lemon wedges to use in place of dressing. Salt and pepper are optional

Perfect Rice

This rice is...perfect!

1 **cup** short or long grain
brown rice
1/2 tsp. extra virgin olive oil

Few drops of water
Salt and pepper or soy sauce,
to taste

Cook rice as directed on package. Add remaining ingredients and mix. Yield: 4 servings.

Note: For softer rice, add 1/4 cup extra water or non-fat chicken broth before cooking.

Per serving:

Calories: 116.3	Protein: 2.4g	Carbohydrates: 24.1g	Fat: 2.0g

Creamy Fruit Salad

Perfect summer food!

1 **cup** mixed fruit, chopped
(See: "Recommended
Products/Shopping List,
p. 101)
1/4 cup nonfat plain or
vanilla yogurt

1/4 tsp. fructose (optional)
2 tsp. orange or apple juice
concentrate
1/4 Tbsp. vanilla (optional)
Raw nuts (optional)

Combine all ingredients. Let stand 15 minutes before serving. Yield: 2 servings.

Per serving:

Calories: 139.8	Protein: 3.4g	Carbohydrates: 32.9g	Fat: 0.3g

Fruit Salad

Eat as a snack or a perfect addition to any meal.

4 **cups** raw, fresh fruit, cubed or
sliced (e.g., bananas, kiwi,
apples, pears, nectarines,
peaches, grapes, pineapple)

2 Tbsp. fresh lemon juice
1 Tbsp. fructose
Raw pecans, chopped (optional)

Stir together lemon juice and fructose; pour over fruit and stir well. (This topping not only tastes good, it also keeps your fruit from turning brown). Optional: add 1/4 cup nonfat plain or vanilla yogurt. Yield: 8 servings.

Per serving:

Calories: 104.9	Protein: 0.4g	Carbohydrates: 25.6g	Fat: 0.1g

Quick Salsa

A terrific taco-topper or baked-chip dip.

1 lb. fresh tomatoes or 1 can (28 oz.) whole tomatoes, finely diced
1 medium yellow onion, chopped
1-2 jalapenos, very finely diced
3 green onions with some chives, chopped
1-2 cloves garlic, minced
1 tsp. salt
1/2 tsp. extra virgin olive oil
2 fresh tomatoes, pureed

Mix all ingredients and refrigerate for at least three hours before serving. Serving size: 1 tablespoon.

Optional ingredients: One can (4 oz.) green chilies or 1/2 avocado, diced.

Per serving:

Calories: 6.1	Protein: 0.2g	Carbohydrates: 1.1g	Fat: 0.1g

Guacamole

Add to any Mexican dish or as a dip for baked corn chips.

1 small avocado, diced
1½ tsp. fresh lemon juice
Dash of cayenne pepper
1/8 tsp. garlic salt
Dash of salt (to taste)

Mash avocado with a fork to desired chunkiness. Add remaining ingredients and stir. If a smooth consistency is desired, mix ingredients in a blender. Hint: Place avocado seed in finished dip to keep dip fresh. Yield: 6 servings.

Per serving:

Calories: 67.7	Protein: 0.7g	Carbohydrates: 2.5g	Fat: 5.1g

Yogurt Cheese

A great alternative to sour cream or cream cheese!

Plain or flavored nonfat yogurt

Place a strainer in a bowl. Empty one container of yogurt into the strainer. Cover and refrigerate for 24 hours. The liquid will drain out, and what remains is yogurt cheese. Yield: 14 servings.

Per serving:

Calories: 8.4	Protein: 0.9g	Carbohydrates: 1.2g	Fat: 0g

Essential Mayo

You'll love the taste of this healthy mayonnaise.

1 egg	1/2 c. olive oil
1 tsp. stone ground mustard	1/2 c. cold pressed safflower oil
2 Tbsp. raw red wine or cider	1/2 tsp. salt
vinegar or fresh lemon juice	Dash pepper

Using a blender or electric mixer, beat first three ingredients at high speed until well blended. Reduce speed to medium and, while still beating, add oils a few drops at a time, gradually, increasing to a thin, steady stream. Beat until it begins to thicken. (Do not overbeat). Add salt and pepper. Serving size: 1 tsp.

Per serving:

Calories: 33	Protein: .1g	Carbohydrates: .04g	Fat: 3.5g

Basic Vinaigrette

Create a special salad-sensation with this dressing.

4 Tbsp. raw red wine vinegar	2 Tbsp. extra virgin olive oil
(can use raw cider vinegar)	1/4 tsp. salt
2 Tbsp. cold pressed	Dash pepper
safflower oil	

Mix all ingredients together. Store in refrigerator. Variations: Add 1 tsp. of any fresh or dried spice (e.g., basil, oregano, or fennel or mustard seeds). Tip: "Basic Vinaigrette" may be added to 6 oz. cooked pasta and one cup chopped, raw vegetables for pasta salad. Serving size: 1 tsp.

Per serving:

Calories: 14.8	Protein: 0g	Carbohydrates: .14g	Fat: 2.3g

For washing fruits and vegetables, fill large bowl or sink with approximately 1/2 gallon water. Add 1/2 Tbsp. white vinegar and, if available, three drops of Infinity²'s ClO_2. Submerge fruits or vegetables for approximately one minute; rinse. Dry and store in air-tight plastic bags. (Small items may be put into a strainer before submerging into water.)

Honey Tarragon Dressing

This blend of honey and tarragon is a winner!

1 **Tbsp.** safflower oil
1 **Tbsp.** olive oil
3 **Tbsp.** raw red wine vinegar
1/2 **tsp.** fresh lemon juice
1 **Tbsp.** fresh orange juice (opt.)
2 **Tbsp.** honey

1 **tsp.** stone ground mustard
(optional)
1/4 **tsp.** garlic salt
1 **tsp.** dried tarragon leaves (opt.
rub leaves between fingers
for fine texture)

Mix all ingredients together. Store in refrigerator. Serving size: 1 tsp.

Tip: Add Yogurt Cheese (p. 87) or mayonnaise made with expeller pressed oils to thicken any dressing. Children often like thicker dressings.

Per serving:

| Calories: 19.0 | Protein: .05g | Carbohydrates: 1.9g | Fat: 1.3g |

Veggie Dip

A healthful party dip.

8 **oz.** plain yogurt or
Yogurt Cheese (p. 87)
1/4 **cup** mayonnaise made with
expeller pressed oils (or use
recipe on p. 88)
2 **Tbsp.** lemon juice
1/2 **tsp.** salt or "No MSG"
Lawry's seasoning

1 **tsp.** garlic powder
1/2 **tsp.** onion powder
1 **tsp.** parsley, ground finely
between fingers or 2 tsp.
dried dill weed
1 **tsp.** raw, organic honey or
maple syrup

Mix all ingredients together. For best results, chill for several hours before serving. Serving size: 1 tsp.

Per serving:

| Calories: 9.24 | Protein: .15g | Carbohydrates: .36g | Fat: .8g |

Drinks

Cinnamon Fruit Shake

Cinnamon adds the perfect touch to this shake.

1/2 **cup** raw skim milk	1/4 **tsp.** cinnamon
2 **Tbsp.** nonfat powdered milk	1 **Tbsp.** apple juice concentrate
2 **cups** fruit (pears, peaches,	1/2 **tsp.** vanilla
cantaloupe, honeydew,	1 **Tbsp.** raw wheat germ
orange, papaya, straw-	
berries, blueberries	
and/or apples)	

Blend ingredients. Serve immediately. Yield: 2 servings.

Per serving:

| Calories: 319.4 | Protein: 9.1g | Carbohydrates: 72.7g | Fat: 1.0g |

Fruity Yogurt Shake

Sweet treat!

1 **cup** fresh or frozen	1 **Tbsp.** raw wheat germ
strawberries, unsweetened	1/2 **tsp.** vanilla
1 **cup** nonfat plain or	1 **tsp.** lime juice
vanilla yogurt	1 **large** banana

Place ingredients in a blender; cover and mix well at medium speed. Serve immediately. Yield: 2 servings.

Per serving:

| Calories: 158.7 | Protein: 8.3g | Carbohydrates: 28.9g | Fat: 1.1g |

Fresh Lemonade

Refreshing on a hot day ... or anytime!

5 **cups** water	1½ **cups** freshly squeezed
3/4 **cups** fructose	lemon juice

Mix all ingredients well and add ice or refrigerate before serving. Yield: 7 servings.

Serving suggestion: Serve with a wedge of lemon or lime on the edge of the glass, or with citrus slices or fresh or frozen strawberries added.

Per serving:

| Calories: 80.6 | Protein: 0.2g | Carbohydrates: 20.5g | Fat: 0.0g |

Tasty Lemon Zing

A "must try."

3-4 **cups** boiling water (depending on strength and sweetness desired)

3 **Tbsp.** fresh lemon juice

3 **Bigelow** "Lemon & C" tea bags (any flavor herb tea may be used)

3 **Tbsp.** fructose

For this recipe, you will need a glass jar or pitcher (approximately 32 oz. size). Pour boiling water into jar. Hang tea bags over the edge. Add remaining ingredients, and stir until fructose is dissolved. With tea bags still hanging out of jar, screw lid on tightly. Refrigerate for several hours, at least until cold. Shake before serving. Yield: 3-4 servings (1 serving = 1 cup).

Per serving:

| Calories: 48.0 | Protein: 0g | Carbohydrates: 12.0g | Fat: 0g |

Other Drinks

Water with lemon wedges

Herb Tea (We recommend Bigelow brand "Orange & C" tea for those who don't generally like tea. It's mild.) Hint: Add 1 tsp. fresh lemon juice and 1 tsp. raw organic honey to any flavor herb tea.

Fresh, raw fruit or vegetable juices (e.g., orange, tangerine, grapefruit, carrot, tomato)

8 oz. warm water with 1 Tbsp. raw vinegar and 2 tsp. raw organic honey

Snacks

Make banana splits or sundaes with fructose-sweetened yogurt (Nanci's Yogurt, if available). Top with fresh or frozen fruits, "chocolate ecstasy" chocolate topping by Newmarket foods (limit to 1 Tbsp. per banana split), and raw nuts. Fruits may be chopped or pureed with a touch of fructose added if desired.

Mix frozen yogurt with fresh or frozen fruits and raw nuts. Try mint yogurt with blueberries or strawberries and raw macadamia nuts or pecans; or French vanilla yogurt with raspberries and slivered almonds.*

Stir 1/4 cup fresh, chilled (almost frozen) orange juice into 3/4 cup vanilla yogurt.

Make frozen juice pops with frozen fresh fruit juice. For variety mix in a little pureed fruit before freezing.

Freeze fruits (e.g., bananas, strawberries, mango, peaches) for a tasty treat.

Eat raw nuts or seeds with raw carrot or celery sticks.

Top celery with raw nut butter.

Dip vegetables (mushrooms, bell peppers, jicama, celery, carrots, sliced yams, etc.) into Veggie dip (p. 89). For dip, use vinegar or lemon juice to dilute 1/2 Tbsp. dressing made with expeller pressed oils. Add salt and pepper.

Snack on fresh fruits, all varieties.

Combine low-fat Knush (Knudsen) cottage cheese with canned fruit.

Make air-popped popcorn.

Top whole wheat crackers with raw cheese.

Spread whole grain breads or whole-grain crackers with non-hydrogenated peanut butter or raw almond butter. Top with raw organic honey or "100% fruit" jelly.

Try nachos p. 66 for a tasty snack.

Infinity² E.N.E.R.G.Y. Bars

Infinity² Fruit Fat-Burner Bars

Remember, enzymes are not destroyed when food is frozen.

Eating Out

The following items are approved choices when eating out:

General Recommendations

Drink herb teas, lemon water or water.
(Take your own tea bag and ask for hot water.)

Eat half raw. You may even want to eat raw vegetables before you go.
If you're tempted by dessert, wait and go out for frozen yogurt.

Avoid alcohol, mineral water, wine spritzers, soda, diet soda, coffee and tea.

Mexican

Corn tortillas, grilled with no oil, or steamed; in place of fried chips

Salsa

Guacamole and/or sliced avocado

Extra lettuce and tomatoes on the side to add nutritional
value without adding calories or fat .

Whole pinto or black beans in place of refried beans

Chicken, fish, shrimp or vegetable fajitas
(Ask for corn or wheat tortillas, grilled or steamed with no oil,
instead of white flour tortillas. Corn tortillas have the least fat.)

Chicken soft tacos with corn tortillas grilled with no oil and no cheese.

For a "legal" burrito, order your choice of whole beans, lettuce,
tomatoes, guacamole or avocados, and grilled whole wheat
or corn tortillas, and make your own.

Avoid chips, nachos, refried beans, beef, fried entrees, sour cream and
cheese. Replace sour cream with extra guacamole.

Oriental

Brown rice, if available

Steamed rice, not fried

Dishes containing vegetables and lean meats that are not deep fried.
(Stir fried is better than deep fried.)

Most soups are fine; however, if you can see oil on the top,
skim it off with the back of your spoon.

Avoid won tons, egg rolls, sweet and sour dishes and fried rice. Also,
tofu should be avoided as it is generally very high in fat.

Italian

Whole wheat or spinach pastas

Clear white sauces, not creamy white sauces

Marinara or tomato sauces (with vegetables, if available)

Lean meats such as clams, shrimp, lobster, oysters and chicken.

Avoid cheese-filled pastas, sausage dishes, cream or butter sauces, veal
parmesan, cheese or beef ravioli and beef lasagna.

American

Grilled, steamed or baked lean meats (e.g., chicken, fish, lobster, crab legs, shrimp)

Salads with lean meats, all vegetables, boiled egg whites.
No yolks, imitation bacon-flavored bits, croutons or cheese.

For salad dressing, use lemon juice, vinegar and/or salt and pepper.
Or, order a dressing on the side, and dilute it with lemon juice
or vinegar. Dip your fork in the dressing before each bite.

Whole grain breads with no butter

Steamed vegetables with no butter or creamy sauces

Non-creamy soups (If fat is on the top, remove it with the back of your spoon.)

Whole bean soups (If the soup has meat,
eat the beans but leave the meat and avoid extra fats.)

Baked potatoes (Order sliced avocado and lemon wedges, or steamed
vegetables to flavor the potato. Or, before you add salt and pepper,
add drops of water or low-fat soup broth, to replenish some moisture.)

Cocktail sauce, lemon wedges

Limit tarter sauce or melted butter sauce (usually comes with
lobster and crab legs) to approximately 1 tsp. and dilute it
with lemon juice or vinegar. Add salt and pepper as desired.

Shish kabobs with lean meats (listed above) and vegetables

Avoid french fries, gravies or sauces, fried chicken or buffalo wings,
potato skins and fatty toppings for potatoes or salads.

Breakfast

Omelets made with egg whites and vegetables

Whole wheat toast, dry

Whole grain pancakes and/or waffles

Low fat yogurt with fresh fruit and approximately 1 Tbsp. granola

Oatmeal or "legal" dry cereal (See list p. 103) with skim milk.

Fresh fruit

Avoid sausage, bacon, ham, and fried hash browns.

The Complete Physique Kitchen

The following guidelines will help you fully implement the *Complete Physique* Nutrition Plan, and thus create a lifestyle of healthy eating. By setting up a *Complete Physique* kitchen, you will have easy access to the healthiest, most nutritious options. Read this entire section. It contains valuable information for food selection, even if you don't do a lot of cooking at home.

As you read this section, place an "X" in the box beside any step you have already taken. Then, circle the box beside the step you would like to take next. Set goals to complete each step, starting with the one that seems easiest and doing the hardest last.

☐ **Throw away** any *bleached* white flour you may have and vow never to buy it again. (White flour is bad, bleached flour is even worse!) Many nutritionists estimate that bleached white flour is four times as hazardous to your health as white sugar.

☐ **Replace refined,** "non-food" items with healthy foods:

Get rid of:	Replace with:
White flour whether bleached or enriched, unbleached flour	*Whole wheat pastry flour, oat flour (p. 84) and other whole grain flours
All carbonated beverages	Any of the drinks listed on p. 90 and 91 (Try them all and repeat your favorites.)
Margarine	"Easy Spread" (p. 84)
Hydrogenated oils	Butter, when cooking (See p. 99 for more details about using oils.)
Refined oils essentially any of the oils that are mass produced and most commonly found on grocery store shelves	Extra virgin olive oil, cold-pressed oils (e.g., canola oil, safflower oil — expeller pressed and "unrefined" oils). (See p. 103 for details.)

☐ **Look through the "Recommended Products/Shopping List (p. 101)."** As you use up the inferior, refined items in your refrigerator, replace them with the least refined (raw when possible) variety. (e.g., Replace apple cider vinegar with "raw" apple cider vinegar.)

☐ **Make a new recipe file box** by following these steps:

☐ Purchase several blank or lined either 3x5 or 4x6 in. index cards, a set of tabbed index cards (with blank tabs) and a new recipe file box.

☐ On the tabbed index cards, write your choice of sections. (Recommended sections are: Breakfast, Main Dishes, Side Dishes, Snacks and/or Fun Recipes for Kids, Drinks, Shopping Lists.) Place your blank index cards at the front or the back of your recipe box, for quick access when you need to record a recipe.

☐ As you try the recipes in *Complete Physique* and gather others that fit with the *Complete Physique* Nutrition Plan criteria (Refer to the Nutrition chapter, record the recipes on cards, then file them in the appropriate section in your file box. If you choose, as you make recipe cards for the *Complete Physique* recipes, you may want to note that you have done so beside the recipe in the book. Since the recipes in this book give many options, record the options you like best on your recipe cards. This will enable you to customize each recipe to fit your individual tastes.

☐ Start new shopping lists on index cards to be placed in your "Shopping Lists" section. Each time you record a new recipe, place the ingredients needed for that recipe on the appropriate shopping list. This will save you a great deal of time because it will eliminate trips back to the store for forgotten items.

☐ Once you have enough recipes for a two-week menu, you will simply need to keep the items on your newly created shopping lists in stock in order to have all of the ingredients you need to prepare your meals and snacks.

☐ Make a card for each place of business where you purchase food items, e.g., the "grocery store," "health food store," "bakery" or "fruit stand." You may also want to have a card for items you order by mail or telephone on a regular basis. On these cards, record any pertinent information such as prices, address, phone number, ID or membership number etc.

Please Note: The shopping lists in your recipe file will not be lists to take to the store, but rather "master" shopping lists which you will use in order to check your kitchen's current food supply and make a shopping list of things you will need to purchase. (See also Recommended Products/Shopping List p. 101)

Complete Physique: Recipes

☐ **Create your own ready-reference Master Menu.** Start with a large piece of card-stock or small poster board. Make spaces for breakfasts, lunches, dinners, fast food, and restaurant options. Fill in the headings, but leave the actual boxes empty. Then, as you find a recipe, meal, or snack idea that works for you and/or your family, add it to your Master Menu. Keep this menu taped inside one of your cupboards (or another handy place). Note: This is not a typical "Sunday-through-Saturday" type menu. Instead, it is a list of recipe ideas that you can refer to when you're preparing meals and a shopping list.

☐ **Purchase cooking tools that will enable you to use healthy,** low fat cooking methods. (You may want to purchase one item at a time and get in the habit of using that item before purchasing another one.)

Suggested Cooking Tools:

- **Spray bottle** for water which can be used in place of oils to keep moisture in foods such as grilled sandwiches, French toast, pancakes — any food being cooked in frying pan. The water can be sprayed directly on the food and the pan. It will evaporate, and will keep the food from losing too much of its own moisture.

- **Strainer/colander** with very fine holes for rinsing excess fat from cooked meats such as ground beef. (Ground chicken breast is preferable and generally needs no rinsing.)

- **Non-stick** stainless steel and cast iron pots are recommended.

- **Rice cooker**/vegetable steamer.

- **Citrus juicer.**

- **Fruit and vegetable juicer.** Even very busy people can find time to juice in bulk and freeze juices in zip-lock freezer bags or glass jars when they realize the health benefits that can be derived from doing so. (Fruit and vegetable juices can also be purchased in a health food store.)

- **Yogurt strainer** for making Yogurt Cheese (p. 87). These can be found in the houseware sections of finer department stores. Some even come with a container to keep the strainer in while in the refrigerator.

- **Save jars** and bottles and their lids to store homemade dressings, such as "Easy Spread" (p. 84), fresh juices, etc.

- **Fat separator** to separate fat from broths. This item is available at most grocery stores and looks like a measuring cup with a spout at the bottom.

- **Chicken roaster** which roasts chicken on end. This will save you time when a recipe requires basting.

Adding fat to your food selections

Because it is important to include 20 percent fat in your diet, the following represent the "ultimate" or preferred choices for adding fats that are easily digested and used in the body for energy, healthy skin and hair, and optimum functioning of all the body's systems:

Each of the following equals approximately 2 grams of fat or 20 calories from fat:

2 Tbsp. grated raw cheese

2 Tbsp. mashed avocado

1/2 tsp. oil (See list of Recommended fats below)

1/2 tsp. butter

1/2 tsp. mayonnaise (made from expeller-pressed oil)

1 tsp. non-hydrogenated peanut butter

1½ tsp. raw nuts (approximately)

To add fat to your foods, first determine the number of calories and how much fat is already in that food. You should have 2 grams of "good" fat for every 100 calories. For example, if you select a nonfat food that has 80 calories, add 2 grams of fat to equal 20 percent fat. If you select a food that has 90 calories and is 10 percent fat, add one gram of fat to equal 20 percent fat.

Recommended Fats for Various Purposes

- **Sautéing or Stir-frying** (because of their stability)
  - Extra Virgin Olive Oil is first choice
  - Butter only when its taste is preferred
- **Baking**
  - Expeller-pressed safflower oil
  - Or, butter only when its taste is preferred

- **Salads, etc.** (anything that won't be heated)
  - Cold-pressed, refrigerated oil in dark bottles, i.e., walnut, soybean, safflower, sesame-untoasted. ("Flora" brand is good.) If you are used to the tasteless, refined oils on the market, you may have to adjust to these. At first, you may mix them with extra virgin olive oil until you're used to their taste.
- **For spreading onto bread, etc.**
  - "Easy Spread" (p. 84)
- **For obtaining the essential fatty acid**, Linoleic Acid (LA)
  - RAW pumpkin, sesame and sunflower seeds; walnuts; wheat germ; almonds; pecans and avocados.
- **For obtaining the essential fatty acid**, Alpha-Linolenic Acid (LNA)
  - RAW flax seeds, walnuts and wheat germ.
    (Recommended: Use some flax on cereal, salads, etc. daily.)

Note: Keep oils and fats away from light, heat and oxygen as much as possible.

Recommended Products/Shopping

In most of the recipes, and on the following list, the "preferred" choice of each ingredient or grocery item is given. You may chose to use alternatives at first, as you use up the items in your cupboards and transition to a healthy way of eating. However, remember that alternatives are inferior and will not promote health like the listed items. The goal is to use as many "preferred" items as possible.

Items marked with an asterisk (*) are often found only in health food stores. If you can't find what you're looking for in a health food store, always ask, as most stores (especially those that are independently owned) are happy to order items for you.

Remember, you want to chose items "as close to nature" as possible. Use this handy reference as a guide. For the greatest nutrition, remember to select foods in this order:

1. **Raw**

2. **Frozen** ** **or dried** without preservatives and at low temperatures

3. **Bottled raw**

4. **Lightly sweetened**

5. **Baked**

6. **Canned**

7. **Microwaved** — never recommended

*** Freezing does not destroy enzymes.*

Baking Products

- baking powder (non-aluminum)
- cornmeal* (whole, not degermed)
- fructose*
- maple syrup* (pure)
- pancake mix*, whole wheat
- powdered milk, skim
- raw organic honey*
- vanilla (pure)
- wheat flour, whole-grain
- whole wheat pastry flour (for cookies, cakes, etc.)

Bread Products

Choose all whole grain products made with no corn syrup, sugar or preservatives. Best from bakery or health food store.*

- bagels
- hamburger buns, mixed grain
- pita bread
- wheat bread

Canned Beans (or fresh)

- black beans
- kidney beans
- pinto beans
- red beans
- refried beans (fat-free)

Canned Fruit

- apricot halves in juice
- fruit salad in juice
- pineapple in juice
- mandarin oranges in light syrup

Canned Meats/Seafood

- chicken breast
- tuna in water

Canned/Jarred Vegetables

- diced and peeled/ sliced green chilies
- mixed vegetables
- whole tomatoes
- stewed tomatoes (also Mexican style)
- watercress
- corn, whole kernel
- sliced olives
- Clauson pickles (not cooked — in the dairy case)
- jalapeno peppers

Cereals and Breakfast Foods

Any cereal made with whole grain flours that has 2 grams or less fat and 5 grams or less sugar per 100 calories.

- Barbara's Puffins
- Barbara's Shredded Spoonfuls
- Fiber One
- Fiber Wise
- Grape-Nuts
- Shredded Wheat and Bran
- Kashi (not puffed)
- Health Valley Muesli
- Nutri-Grain Nuggets

Condiments

- barbecue sauce
- chili sauce
- mayonnaise made with expeller pressed oils* (can dilute with vinegar or lemon)
- stoneground mustard*
- red-wine and apple cider vinegars* (raw)
- soy sauce* (kind from health food store with no MSG, corn syrups or colorings)
- "100% fruit" jellies
- teriyaki sauce

Oils

- extra virgin olive oil
- cold-pressed safflower oil ("Flora" brand)
- expeller-pressed safflower oil (for use in baking)
- Nature's Cuisine brand All natural Olive spray and Extra Virgin Olive Oil for cooking and seasoning distributed by Nature's Best

Dairy Products

(e.g., *Alta Dena brand — Their cows are not treated with growth hormone.)

- butter (Use butter instead of margarine. Butter made from raw cream is best, and it freezes well.)
- cheddar cheese*, made from raw milk
- cottage cheese, low fat (Knudsen or *Alta Dena Brands are recommended.)
- eggs* (range free)
- egg white
- nonfat plain yogurt*
- skim or whole milk*, raw if possible
- yogurt*, sweetened with fruit juices (e.g. Alta Dena brand)
- frozen yogurt, fructose sweetened (e.g. Nanci's Frozen Yogurt)

Dried Beans and Rice

- beans (e.g. kidney, pinto, etc.)
- brown rice — short, long grain or wild

Drinks

- freshly squeezed fruit and vegetable juices*
- herb teas (e.g. Bigelow "Orange & C," "Lemon & C")

Fresh Fruits

- fresh fruits — all varieties (See p. 49 for Glycemic Index.)
- apples
- lemons
- limes
- bananas
- kiwi
- fruits dried in their own juices with no preservatives* (to be eaten sparingly
- fruit leather* ("100% fruit" variety)

Fresh Seafood

- fish fillets

Frozen Fruit and Juices

- Use frozen concentrate in recipes only. For drinking, select fresh fruit and vegetable juices.
- apple juice, frozen concentrate
- orange juice, frozen concentrate

Frozen Vegetables

- corn
- mixed vegetables
- green beans
- peas
- broccoli

Grain Products

- hot-cooked whole grain/ cracked grain cereals*
- wheat germ* (raw)
- whole grain pancake mix

Infinity² Products

- Definition Powder
- Proteabolic Mass Nutrients
- Proteabolic Protein Powder

Meat, Fish and Poultry

- chicken breasts, skinless, boneless
- deli-sliced chicken and turkey breast (home-cooked/sliced preferred)
- ground chicken breast (See tip p. 67 to make your own.)
- fish fillets, fresh
- ground turkey breast
- whole chicken (hormone or antibiotic-free strongly recommended)
- whole turkey breast, skinless, boneless

Mexican Food Products

- baked corn chips
- corn tortillas no preservatives*
- enchilada sauce
- fat-free refried beans
- picante sauce salsa
- whole wheat tortilla or chapati*

Nuts and Seeds

- slivered almonds (raw)
- nuts (raw)
- pecans (raw)
- pumpkin seeds
- raw nut butters*
- non-hydrogenated peanut butter (e.g. *Arrowhead Mills, Laura Schudder's)
- sunflower seeds (raw)
- flax seeds

Pasta

- all vegetable and whole grain
- bow-tie
- fettuccine
- lasagna noodles
- rotini
- shell pasta
- spaghetti
- ziti pasta

Produce

- all fresh vegetables
- avocado
- banana
- bean sprouts
- broccoli
- cabbage or pre-packaged coleslaw vegetables
- carrots
- celery
- cherry tomatoes
- cucumber
- escarole
- garlic
- green beans
- green chilies
- green onions
- red/green pepper
- lemon juice
- lettuce
- mixed greens
- mushrooms
- onion
- orange juice
- potato
- red onion
- romaine lettuce
- spinach
- strawberries
- sweet potatoes
- tomatillos
- tomato
- watercress
- white potatoes
- yams
- yellow onion
- zucchini

Salad Dressings
- mayonnaise made with expeller pressed oil*
- dressings made with expeller pressed oils

Soups and Gravies
- chicken broth (fat free)
- chicken gravy (Heinz brand fat free)

Spices and Seasonings
Select spices with no MSG. Soy sauce found in health food stores is superior to others that often contain sugars, colorings or MSG.

- parsley, fresh
- basil, fresh
- cayenne pepper
- chili powder
- cinnamon
- Lawry's (No MSG)
- Mrs. Dash
- nutmeg
- vegetable bouillon cubes*
- pepper
- sea salt*
- garlic salt

- lemon pepper
- celery salt
- bay leaves
- Hain brand taco seasoning*
- Hain brand chili seasoning*
- parsley flakes
- oregano
- instant chicken broth and seasoning mix
- Italian seasoning

- garlic powder
- "Butter Buds Sprinkles"*
- natural maple flavoring
- stone ground mustard
- tarragon
- paprika
- cilantro, fresh
- ginger, fresh

Sweetners
- pure crystalline fructose*
- raw organic honey*

Tomato Sauces
- marinara sauce
- spaghetti sauce, nonfat
- tomato paste

- tomato sauce
- pizza sauce

Found most often in health food stores.

Exercise

Including an Easy-to-Follow Workout Routine

Chapter Five

Exercise

Throughout history, even the earliest civilizations sensed the importance of physical activity. Though exercise was often viewed as just a diversion or a way to maintain balance, as early as 400 B.C., Hippocrates taught, *"All parts of the body which have a function, if used in moderation and exercised in labours in which each is accustomed, become thereby healthy, well-developed, and age more slowly, but if unused and left idle, they become liable to disease, defective in growth and age quickly."*[1]

Recent research confirms that exercise does, indeed, have many benefits for health. In fact, physical activity has a positive effect on so many different diseases and conditions that it could almost be considered a "cure-all." Proper and consistent exercise offers a three-prong offensive against such common conditions as arthritis, heart disease, back pain, cancer, diabetes, osteoporosis and obesity. First, exercise decreases the chance of contracting an unhealthy condition in the first place. Next, physical activity supports healing and helps you cope with disease when it is already present. Third, exercise delays the progress of many diseases.

Exercise Your Way to Health

Even more importantly, exercise also contributes to improved quality of life on a day to day basis. Exercise bolsters the immune system, increases energy and alleviates stress, producing the natural endorphins that create a peaceful, euphoric state. Exercisers can relax more completely, even under pressure; and regular physical activity appears to reduce symptoms of depression and anxiety, helping to improve one's mood and ability to perform daily tasks.

However, in order to derive the greatest possible benefits and avoid the negative side effects as discussed in the "Do I Need?" chapter, exercise must be performed properly and consistently. Whatever your current fitness level, your goal should be to begin an exercise program that makes you feel good within a short amount of time and that contributes to long-term health as well. There are many misconceptions about what such a program must include. As discussed earlier, both cardiovascular and resistance exercises are important. However, you will find the approach recommended here is very different than many of the programs that are popular today.

Remember, exercise is not just for athletes, for young people, or for people who are overweight. Exercise is essential for every individual. However, exercise should not be viewed as something we "have" to do. Instead, by exercising properly and approaching workouts with a positive attitude, we can quickly begin to reap the benefits that will keep us enthused about this invaluable aspect of a total program for health.

The program outlined in this chapter has been proven to be comprehensive and health-producing. By adhering to the following guidelines, you will be able to see results quickly, and you will find it easy to continue progressing toward your goal.

Guidelines for Strength Training

There are many ways to approach strength training. The most popular techniques are not necessarily the best. We suggest you throw out any preconceived ideas of what is the right way to perform resistance exercises, because most often, what people do and what the research shows are two different things.

From the time we first opened the Infinity² Fitness Center clinic until today, the emphasis has been on results. We have worked with athletes, business people and busy housewives. These people have careers and families that depend on them feeling good and having health. At Infinity² Fitness Center, we aren't seeking to provide a social club or a playground. Instead, we have created what could be called a "health factory" where people get results. Best of all, we have found ways for you to duplicate those results in your own home or at your local gym.

After thorough research, including in-depth studies in our clinic, we have adopted a technique that has proven to be the most effective and safest way to perform strength training exercises. This technique involves more muscle fiber than other methods, which means more dramatic results can be attained in less exercise time. It's known as Super-Slow. The following guidelines will help you understand how to do Super-Slow correctly and will illustrate how Super-Slow differs from traditional strength training techniques.

Slow, Not Fast

Super-Slow is performed using a very slow movement. We found that the most immediate and dramatic results could be achieved when exercises are performed using a 7/7 count. In other words, the hard part of the exercise (lifting the weight up, or the positive movement) should take seven seconds, and the easy part (returning the weight back down, the negative movement) should take seven seconds. Use this 7/7 count whether you are lifting weights, or whether your body (and gravity!) are supplying the resistance, as in many of the exercises we recommend.

Fitness appears to compensate even for other
risk factors that might shorten life.

Often, in traditional weight lifting programs a count of two seconds up and four seconds down is used. However, the slower, more controlled movements of Super-Slow have been proven to be safer and more effective, providing at least 59 percent better strength gains.[2]

Smooth, Not Jerky

Perform exercises with a smooth, flowing movement, being careful not to stop and rest at the top or bottom. Instead, keep the exercise going. It is also important to breath consistently and constantly with each repetition. Use a Lamaze-type breathing style — breathing in and out of your mouth with deep, even breaths.

Brief, Not Long

A typical workout session should last only 20 minutes. There are two advantages to keeping your workouts short. First, you will find it easier to consistently schedule time to work out. Second, it actually does your body more harm than good to work out for long periods of time. If you exercise more than 45 minutes to an hour, the body begins to produce increased amounts of cortisol, the hormone that "eats" the muscle you are trying to create![3]

Focused repetitions, not haphazard

Although brief, your workout should be challenging and intense. One set of focused, quality repetitions can accomplish much more than multiple sets using a haphazard approach. To make each repetition a "quality" repetition:

- **Keep** your breathing consistent

- **Focus** on the particular muscle you are working

- **Always** maintain good form. (See illustrations and descriptions of each exercise in this section.)

- **Above all**, make sure you perform each exercise to complete muscle fatigue.

Muscle fatigue means to the point that it is impossible to do another repetition in good form. Completely fatiguing the muscle is necessary in order to see results. The exciting thing about this kind of exercise is that usually, by the very next session, you will see improvement and you will be able to perform more repetitions or will need to increase the resistance for that exercise in order to reach fatigue.

Thus, to maintain consistent results from your strength training, the amount of time you work out does not need to increase. Instead, you will increase the amount of resistance (weight) if necessary. Each of the exercises that are illustrated in this section teach you how to start if you are a beginner, and also how to increase the intensity of the exercise. You may eventually want to add dumbbells or barbells to your home workout equipment; however, some people simply use household objects such as soup cans or plastic milk jugs filled with water to increase the resistance.

Every other day, not daily

While many people think it is beneficial to do strength training daily, this isn't true. When you exercise using resistance, you break the muscle fibers down, and they need a day to rest and to rebuild themselves. This is how your strength increases, by breaking those fibers down and then allowing them to recover.

Some people think they should work one set of muscles at a time — leg muscles one day and arms the next, for example. This is not the case. The body is a dynamic machine that functions best when all parts are working synergistically. Rather than working different muscle groups each day, as some programs suggest, you will find that the body works best when you exercise all muscles of the body to fatigue on the same day, and then allow them to rest for a day.

This is perhaps one of the most important of these recommendations. Perform the resistance exercises outlined in this book every other day, i.e. Monday, Wednesday and Friday or Tuesday, Thursday and Saturday. On the three "off-days" do cardiovascular exercise, applying the guidelines in this chapter. Then, one day a week, rest completely from any exercise.

Simple, not complicated

The Super-Slow routine included in this book is very simple. It focuses on the major muscle groups, including exercises that are biomechanically correct, or in other words, exercises that comply with and encourage the body's normal range of movement.

With the *Complete Physique* exercise program, you won't be doing daily, long, complicated, haphazard workouts of fast, jerky exercises. Instead, you will be following a simple routine of slow, smooth exercises in brief, but intense, sessions every other day.

- **Slow**, not fast
- **Smooth**, not jerky
- **Brief**, not long
- **Focused repetitions**, not haphazard
- **Every other day**, not daily
- **Simple**, not complicated

Performing the suggested exercises properly, in 20-minute sessions three times a week will yield exciting results in terms of greater fitness, shapeliness, health and vitality. If you haven't done so already, complete the assessment in the Appendix so you have a beginning point for monitoring your progress. Also, you may want to make several photocopies of the workout chart found on page 133, so you can use this chart to track your strength-training workouts.

Before you begin, be sure to create a mental picture of what you want to achieve by following the instructions in the Envision chapter.

Then, begin today to follow the *Complete Physique* workout program! See pages 119-132 for complete instructions for each exercise.

Cardiovascular Exercise Guidelines

Strength training alone offers some cardiovascular benefit and provides an important foundation for health. Adding cardiovascular training to your exercise regimen, if done properly can further promote health. For example, studies prove that cardiovascular exercise increases 'good' cholesterol (HDL), decreases the risk of heart disease, lowers blood pressure and may reduce  the incidence of some cancers. Cardiovascular exercise also helps prevent adult-onset diabetes, particularly in those at highest risk.

In a recent study, researchers learned that a change from sedentary living to active living, even late in life, provides almost immediate health improvements. "among middle-aged Harvard male alumni who were sedentary in 1962 or 1966, those who took up moderately intense sports activity during the study's 11 years of follow-up had a 23 percent lower death rate than those who remained sedentary. ...added years of life were observed in all age groups including men 75-84 years of age".[5]

Interestingly, this study showed that "those who became fit had a significant 64 percent reduction in their relative mortality rate. In comparison, men who stopped smoking reduced their [mortality rate] by about 50 percent." In other words, it was even more beneficial for these men to increase activity than to quit smoking.[6]

Avoiding Cardiovascular Abuse

For years, the positive aspects of cardiovascular exercise have been recognized, yet many people abuse this type of exercise. Apparently, most of us don't fully understand how to get the benefits we desire from cardiovascular exercise.

Most people who choose to do cardiovascular exercise have one primary goal and that is to lose weight, which means they need to burn fat. The problem is that most people maintain a heart rate that is much too high during their work out. As a result, they burn more carbohydrates than fat. Others are exercising at a heart rate that is too low, so they are not burning enough calories and are not able to increase their metabolism. Discouraged, yet determined to get results, many exercisers often increase the length of time they exercise or the exercise intensity. The result has been a higher incidence of injury and unhealthy side effects, such as depression and eating disorders.

Because of recent research, we recommend interval training as the most effective way to do cardiovascular exercise. Interval training is an effective exercise technique that varies the intensity of your workout both during the workout and throughout the week. This approach will yield the results that people have been looking for from this type of exercise.

During an interval workout you alternate the time spend at a low heart rate (or low-intensity, fat-burning zone) and the time spent at a higher heart rate, which is your high-intensity, calorie-burning zone that effectively raises your metabolism. It is also important to alternate your workouts throughout the week and allow for proper recovery. To accomplish this you rotate low, medium and high-intensity workouts during the week.

Calculate Your "Target Heart Rate"

Let us explain. The most effective way to do cardiovascular exercise is to keep the heart rate at what is known as your "target heart rate.". To figure your target heart rate, subtract your age from 220. That sum is your maximum heart rate.

To stay in the "safe zone", where the body burns equal amounts of fat and carbohydrates, the heart rate must be kept much lower while doing cardiovascular exercise. The target rate at which you will burn half carbohydrates and half fat is 60 to 65 percent (or lower) of your maximum heart rate. Anytime exercise is performed at a higher heart rate, less fat is burned while more carbohydrates are used to fuel the body. When exercising at 60 percent, you should be able to carry on a conversation with another individual. This is your zone 1, recovery zone or "fat-burning" zone.

The next exercise zone is the "anaerobic threshold". This zone is at approximately 80 to 85 percent of your maximum heart rate. In this zone you are utilizing primarily carbohydrates for fuel, but you are increasing the number of calories burned and increasing your cardio-vascular endurance. The third zone is the Peak Training Zone. The peak zone is approximately 85 to 90 percent of your maximum heart rate. Training in this zone will help increase metabolism, however, this zone should be used only after you have developed a strong base fitness level.

Most individuals should begin an exercise program by utilizing their "fat-burning" zone. Unfortunately, most aerobic exercise, including active sports, often raises the heart rate beyond 65 percent. But now, because of an exciting breakthrough, we have found a way that allows people to exercise at a higher rate (up to 80 percent) while still burning the desired fat. Using a machine called a metabolic cart, we can measure Respiratory Exchange Rate (RER), a measurement that indicates whether the body is burning more fat or carbohydrates. In a

Target Heart Rate
(Percent of Maximum)

Age	60%	80%	Age	60%	80%
under 20	126	168	50	102	136
20	120	160	55	99	132
25	117	156	60	96	128
30	114	152	65	93	124
35	111	148	70	90	120
40	108	144	75	87	116
45	105	140	80	84	112

study conducted by an exercise physiologist, 45 people were tested on this machine. They were then given a supplement, which contains fat digesting enzymes and other supporting nutrients (Lipo-chromizyme). By using this supplement to help digest fat and balance the body, the test showed that people were able to exercise at a higher heart rate (up to 80 percent) and still be burning as much fat as they did at 60 percent.

How to take your heart rate:

1. Pause during physical activity and take your pulse by first locating the artery in your wrist or neck. To locate the artery in your wrist, with one palm facing up, place the index and middle fingers of your other hand on the thumb side of your wrist. Apply light pressure. To locate the artery in your neck, place your index and middle fingers at the base of the ear, just behind the jawbone. Slide the fingers downward to the underside of the jaw, until your fingers are almost to the middle of the neck. Apply light pressure.

2. Count your pulse for 10 seconds, and then use the conversion chart below to determine the total beats per minute.

3. Find your 60 percent "safe zone" Increase or decrease the intensity of your aerobic exercise as needed to stay at your target heart rate. (You increase intensity when you increase speed or use more arm movements, step higher, etc. - any movement that makes the exercise "harder.")

Ten-Second Heart Rate

10-Second Count	Beats Per Minute	10-Second Count	Beats Per Minute	10-Second Count	Beats Per Minute
8	48	17	102	26	156
9	54	18	108	27	162
10	60	19	114	28	168
11	66	20	120	29	174
12	72	21	126	30	180
13	78	22	132	31	186
14	84	23	138	32	192
15	90	24	144	33	198
16	96	25	150	34	204

Amazing benefits can come from the combination of superslow strength training and moderate intensity cardiovascular training, particularly when Lipo-chromizyme is used during cardiovascular exercise. Follow these guidelines for properly adding cardiovascular exercise to your complete exercise program:

Incorporate Interval Training
Alternate the time spent at a low heart rate (or low-intensity, fat-burning zone) and the time spent at a higher heart rate, which is your high-intensity, calorie-burning zone that effectively raises your metabolism. It is also important to alternate your workouts throughout the week and allow for proper recovery. To accomplish this you rotate low, medium and high-intensity workouts during the week.

Vary activity, don't repeat
Every three or four weeks, vary the cardiovascular activity. It will be beneficial for you to cross-train in this way in order to avoid burnout and decrease the possibilities of injury, while you continue to see results.

Below is a list of cardiovascular exercises and the number of calories, which can be burned while doing that particular exercise. Remember, if you keep your heart rate at 60 percent, half of the calories you burn will come from fat. If you do cardio-vascular exercise that increases the heart rate up to 80 percent, take two Lipo-chromizyme 15 to 20 minutes before you exercise in order to maintain the fat-burning capability.

Calories Burned in 30 minutes

Activity	Your Weight (LBS)								
	100	125	150	175	200	250	275	300	350
Aerobic Dancing 182	218	254	290	326	398	434	470	542	
Bicycling (12 MPH) 170	200	230	260	290	350	380	410	470	
Golf (Walking) 85	106	127	148	169	211	232	253	295	
Jogging (10 min./mile) . 210	250	290	330	370	450	490	530	610	
Racquetball 190	228	266	304	342	418	456	494	570	
Skiing (Cross Country) . . 200	242	284	326	368	452	494	536	620	
Stair Climbing 220	266	312	358	404	496	542	588	680	
Swimming (40 yds/min.) 150	180	210	240	270	330	360	390	450	
Walking 135	163	191	219	247	303	331	359	415	
Tennis (Singles) 140	170	200	230	260	320	350	380	440	

Chapter Five: Exercise

Active, not intense

Remember, your goal when doing cardiovascular exercise is to be active and to keep your body moving. It's not to increase strength. Because you will be performing cardiovascular exercises on the days when your muscles should be resting from your strength-training workouts, you shouldn't add weights or other kinds of resistance to your cardiovascular routines. High-intensity cardiovascular aerobics, such as step aerobics, don't allow the muscles to recuperate like they need to: Find an aerobic activity that is relaxing and fun!

A Dynamic Duo

This two-technique combination of strength-training and cardiovascular exercise is highly effective. Be sure to include both techniques and to perform the exercises properly. "if resistance exercise is not performed to complement the cardiovascular program, muscle loss will likely occur. ... If caloric intake is not reduced in the presence of muscle loss, unneeded calories will be stored as fat."[7]

You will be pleased to find how easily and quickly you are able to see and feel results as you follow this Complete Physique program. The change in your current activity level need not be dramatic. As stated in the 1996 Surgeon General's report, "modest increases in physical activity are likely to be more achievable and sustainable for sedentary people than are more drastic changes, and it is sedentary people who are at greatest risk for poor health related to inactivity."[8] Overall, the report emphasizes the importance of "activity of at least a moderate amount on a regular basis."[9]

Don't wait another day to begin your renewal and rejuvenation, and to start claiming the health benefits you deserve.

Good health and permanent weight loss can only be obtained when a sensible diet is combined with a proper exercise program.

Workout

1. **Always breathe consistently** during the full movement of each repetition.

2. **Perform each exercise using the 7/7 count** (seven seconds up and seven seconds down).

3. **Perform each exercise to failure** — or in other words for as many repetitions as you can with proper form, up to 15 repetitions. After you can do 15 repetitions with good form using the 7/7 count, add resistance. (The "crunches" exercise is the only exception to the 15-rep rule. Do as many crunches as you can each workout.)

4. **Do this workout three days a week** on alternating days. This exercise routine can be done even when traveling or on vacation.

5. **Add cardiovascular exercise to your strength training regimen** by doing at least 20 to 30 minutes of properly performed aerobics three times a week. (See the cardiovascular training guidelines on page 113 for more complete instructions.)

6. **Use the workout chart** to track your progress.

7. **Be consistent with your workouts.** Make your health a priority by doing whatever it takes to arrange your schedule so you can include time to exercise.

Other hints:

To derive optimum benefit from your workouts, always try to get at least seven hours of sleep each night.

You will experience greater results if your nutrition is balanced. Follow the *Complete Physique* Nutrition Plan and the suggestions for replenishment.

Standing Squat

This is the best overall exercise for the lower body. It will help strengthen the front and back of the legs (quadraceps and hamstrings); and because these are the largest muscles in the body, Standing Squats will help raise the metabolism significantly.

Instructions:

Stand upright with your feet shoulder-width apart, toes pointing forward or slightly outward. Keeping the back straight and bending the knees, squat down in seven seconds, until the thigh is parallel to the floor. Make sure that you stay flat-footed. (You might need to compensate for leaning forward or back in order to maintain your balance by rotating your hip backwards or leaning your shoulders forward.) Go back to an upright position, utilizing a seven-second count. Do not lock the knees out at the top, but immediately start the downward motion, again using a seven-second count. Perform this exercise to failure or 15 repetitions.

Beginners: Hold on to the back of a chair for balance. Squat down as low as possible, even if you can't go to parallel. Do as many repetitions as you can (to failure).

Advanced: When you can do 15 repetitions using the slow technique and maintaining good form throughout, add hand weights for more resistance.

Stand upright.

Squat down.

Duck Squat

This exercise isolates the inner thighs, helping to shape and strengthen the adductors. It also helps to work all of the leg muscles.

Instructions:

Stand upright, with the heels approximately 24 inches apart and the toes pointing outward. Place a two-by-six inch board or thick phone book under the heels to elevate them. Keeping the back straight and bending the knees, squat down in seven seconds until the thighs are parallel to the floor, and then, taking seven seconds, slowly return to a standing position. Do not lock your knees out at the top, but immediately start the downward motion again. Remember to breathe constantly throughout the exercise.

Beginners: Hold on to the back of a chair for balance. Even if you can't go all the way to parallel, squat down as far as possible and do as many repetitions as you can. Your strength will soon increase until you are able go down all the way and add more repetitions.

Advanced: Add resistance by holding weights in each hand.

Stand upright.

Squat down.

Lunges

This exercise will isolate the hamstring and gluteal muscles, helping to raise and firm the buttocks. This is a great shaping exercise.

Instruction:

Standing at one end of a room, step forward with one foot, using a slightly longer than normal step. Allow the knee of the trailing leg to lower until the knee almost touches the floor, without the front knee going out over the front toe. Stand up slightly, and bring the trailing leg forward slowly, taking another step without resting in the middle; again allow the back leg to lower until the knee almost touches the floor. Continue this lunging motion across the room, and then turn around and go back. This movement does not use the Super-Slow count but should be done slowly and smoothly. Maintain good posture, making sure the head and shoulders are upright.

Beginners: Add lunges after you have been on the Complete Physique Workout for two weeks. Do one length of the room when you first start and gradually work up until you can do two lengths.

Advanced: Add hand weights. Also, each time, after the knee is lowered toward the ground, lift the trailing leg up off the floor behind you until the foot is waist-high (or as high as you can lift it without hyperextending the back); then swing that leg forward to continue the lunging motion.

Stand upright.

Step forward and lower the back knee.

Standing Calf Raises

The Calf Raise exercise will strengthen and shape the calves and will allow for more range of motion in the ankle. It will also help add endurance for walking or jogging.

Instruction:

Place the balls of the feet on the edge of a two-by-six inch board or on the edge of a step, with the heels hanging off the edge. Lock the knees, and balance the body by holding onto a chair or stair rail. Gradually raise the heels to a count of seven seconds until you are standing on your tiptoes. Be sure to extend up as high as possible. Lower the heels in seven seconds, until a deep stretch is achieved.

Advanced: Once you can do 15 repetitions, perform this exercise by standing on one leg and proceeding as explained above. Repeat with the other leg.

Heels down.

Raise heels.

Kneeling Leg Lift

This exercise works the upper gluteals, to help shape and achieve a roundness to this area of the body.

Instruction:

Place knees and hands on the floor, keeping the back straight so shoulders are parallel to the hips. Using seven seconds to complete the motion, keeping the knee bent at a right angle, extend one leg back and up, until the thigh is parallel to the floor. Squeeze and flex the leg and buttocks at the top of the motion. In seven seconds, lower the leg back to the kneeling position. Perform the same motion with the other leg, continuing to perform the upward motion in seven seconds and the downward in seven. Do as many as possible, up to 15 on each leg.

Kneeling position.

Extend leg up.

Push-up

Push-ups work the chest, shoulders and upper arms. Push-ups help greatly with posture, strength and shape.

Instruction:

With this exercise, there are several ways to start easily and then progress. Most people should start this exercise using a negative-only technique. Assume a standard push-up position on the toes with hands and body stiff. The hands should be placed slightly wider than shoulder-width. Lower the body to the floor by slowly bending the arms to a count of seven seconds. Do not try to push yourself up into the top position. When you reach the floor, bend the knees, straighten the arms and get back onto the toes and stiffen the body once again. Begin another repetition, lowering yourself in seven seconds. **Note:** If you cannot do at least five push-ups slowly from this position, then perform them from the knees, keeping the back stiff and straight. Whether you are doing push-ups from your toes or your knees, when you can do 15 without becoming fatigued, change the exercise to include the positive movement (pushing up). Lower the body in seven seconds and then raise it again in seven seconds.

Beginners: See note above. For many beginners, it is best to do push-ups on a bed, to allow for a softer "landing." If you are unable to hold the body up to perform the push-up as described above, begin by lying on the stomach with the hands near the shoulders, slightly wider than shoulder-width apart; then, push-up the entire body as high as possible. Lower, and repeat. Again, as with the other exercises, do what you can. Your strength will improve rapidly if you do these exercises consistently.

Assume push-up position.

Lower to the floor.

Door Row

Perform these exercises to strengthen the back muscles. This will improve posture and help to stabilize the spinal discs in the back, helping to prevent injury.

Instructions:

Roll up a towel and grab it with your hands near the middle of the towel, about six inches apart. Facing the narrow edge of an open door, place the middle of the towel against the door's edge just above the door knobs. Loop the ends of the towel around the knobs on each side. Slide the hands down to the end of the towel, and place the feet on either side of the door. Lean the torso down and back, and bend at the knees so thighs are parallel with the floor and the arms are extended. Stay in this position, keeping your torso angled away from the door. Keeping the elbows in, and using a 7-second count, pull yourself up until the chest meets the hands. Flex the back muscles. Lower yourself back down in seven seconds. You can control the amount of resistance by altering the angle of your torso (the more you lean back). Do as many as possible, maintaining good form, up to 15.

With a partner: Face your partner, each of you holding onto one end of a towel with both hands, palms facing the floor. Extend the arms straight out toward your partner. Your partner should have the hands in close to the body. Pull the towel toward you, while your partner opposes the motion. Your partner's arms should now be extended and your arms should be in close to your body. Repeat the motion, this time with your partner pulling in while you resist the motion.

Door rows or partner rows can be used in place of or alternated with lat pull downs. See page 127.

Lean down and back.

Pull forward.

Lat Pull Down

To strengthen the back muscles, Lat pull downs can be used in place of, or alternated with, the door row or partner row.

Instruction:

You will need a towel and a partner. Sit backward on a chair, with the hands high above the head, holding the ends of the rolled-up towel. Have your partner hold the middle of the towel. While your partner provides continuous resistance by pulling up, pull the towel down behind your head in a slow smooth motion (seven-second count). Have your partner then reverse the resistance by pulling down while you push the towel back up to the starting position, again in seven seconds. Continue to fatigue or to 15 repetitions.

Hands above head.

Pull down.

Tricep Extension

This exercise will strengthen and build the tricep muscle.

Instruction:

For the Seated Tricep Extension, you will need two chairs. Start with the heels on one chair and place the other chair far enough away so that the palms of the hands are on the edge of the chair just behind the body, slightly more than shoulder-width apart. Keep the body upright. There should be a parallel line between the heels, the hips and the palms of hands. Lower the body in seven seconds until the shoulders are parallel with the elbows, then raise the body back up in seven seconds. At the top of the motion, squeeze the triceps and then immediately begin to lower using the seven-second count.

An alternative that works the triceps is the Towel Tricep Extension. By yourself, hold onto one end of the towel behind your head with one hand and holding the other end of the towel with your other hand behind your back. One hand will provide the downward resistance while the other hand pulls up. Switch hands and repeat the motion.

With a partner: Hold on to the center of a rolled-up towel with both hands, with the hands close together and the elbows in. Begin with your hands behind your head and have your partner hold on to the ends of the towel. Pull up on the towel, extending your arms in seven seconds while your partner pulls down to provide resistance.

Beginners: The Seated Tricep Extension exercise is difficult, even for individuals who are more advanced. Make it easier by performing it as described above but with the feet on the floor rather than up on another chair.

Heels on chair.

Lower the body.

Arm Curl

Performing Arm Curls will create a great looking bicep that will add to the arm strength and to the overall fitness and look of the body.

Instruction:

Stand erect with a weight in each hand. Hold the elbows close to the sides, never allowing the arms to move behind the body. Bending at the elbow, curl the weights up to the shoulders in seven seconds; then, lower again in seven seconds. It is important to maintain good posture and not swing the arms from side to side or to arch the back while performing this exercise. When you can do 15 repetitions increase the resistance by adding more weight or working with a partner as described below.

With a partner: If you are working with a partner, do the Towel Arm Curl. Hold on to a rolled-up towel, with hands slightly less than shoulder-width apart in front of you, palms facing up. Have your partner face you, holding on to the ends of the towel. Begin with your arms down, and curl up to your shoulders in a seven-second count while your partner opposes your motion by pulling down on the ends of the towel. Then, reverse the motion, pulling the towel down and returning the hands to the side, while your partner continues to supply resistance.

Hold elbows close to sides.   *Curl weights up.*

Lateral Raise

Performing this exercise correctly will add shape to the deltoid muscle, helping the waist appear smaller and more proportionate.

Instruction:

Stand erect with the arms at your sides and a weight in each hand. Keeping the arms straight with the wrists slightly curled under, raise weights to just above shoulder height in seven seconds. Pause, then lower smoothly in seven seconds. As mentioned previously, household items can be used for weights, such as soup cans or gallon cartons filled with different amounts of water to vary resistance. Increase the weight when you are able to do 15 slow repetitions in good form.

Beginner: If necessary, begin the exercise without weights. Stand erect. Lift the arms slowly, and then lower them to the sides, doing each movement in seven seconds. Add weights as soon as you are able.

Stand erect, arms at sides.

Lift smoothly.

Military Press

To work and add shape to the deltoid muscle, the Military Press can be used in place of, or alternated with, lateral raises. (See p. 130.)

Instruction:

Hold a rolled up towel with hands slightly more than shoulder-width apart. Have your partner hold the ends of the towel. Begin with your hands just above your shoulders, towel behind your head. Push up, extending but not fully straightening your arms, in a seven second count, while your partner opposes the motion by pulling down on the ends of the towel. Then, reverse the motion, pulling the towel down and returning the hands to the side, while your partner continues to supply resistance. Continue to fatigue or 15 repetitions.

Hands above head.

Pull down.

Crunches

Unlike sit-ups which can sometimes hurt the back, Crunches isolate only the abdominals. They are great for sculpting a firm stomach.

Instruction:

Lie face up on the floor with the hands on the stomach. Bring the heels to within two feet of the buttocks, and raise the toes off the ground. From this position, lift the shoulders and back off the floor as high as possible keeping the chin up and the neck straight. Try to hold the highest position for seven seconds. You will notice that only about a third of a standard sit-up is being performed. Lower the shoulders and the back to the floor in seven seconds. Continue, doing as many crunches as possible. Unlike the other exercises, crunches may be done daily.

Lie face up.

Lift shoulders and back off floor.

Name _____

Date

Body Weight

☐ Male ☐ Female Age _____ Height _____

Standing Squat		
Duck Squat		
Lunges		
Standing Calf		
Kneeling Leg		
Push-up		
Door-row		
Tricep Extension		
Arm Curl		
Lateral Raise		
Crunches		

Name _____ ☐ Male ☐ Female Age _____ Height _____

Date																			
Body Weight																			
Standing Squat																			
Duck Squat																			
Lunges																			
Standing Calf																			
Kneeling Leg																			
Push-up																			
Door-row																			
Tricep Extension																			
Arm Curl																			
Lateral Raise																			
Crunches																			

Replenishment

Chapter Six

Replenishment

Represented by the "R" in the E.N.E.R.G.Y.™ acronym, replenishment refers to replacing, or adding back, the vitamins, minerals, antioxidants, flora and enzymes, which are missing due to lifestyle and environmental factors.

Statistics show that over 90 percent of the population are deficient in some vitamin and/or mineral.[1] Supplementation (replenishment) is the only way to ensure optimum health, vitality and longevity.

As explained in the "Do I Need" chapter, virtually every individual has the same foundational replenishment needs. This chapter will focus on the products that will best meet those needs. A simple "How Much Do I Need?" questionnaire will help you determine how much supplementation is appropriate for you. This questionnaire will also help you identify lifestyle habits that can be changed so you can decrease the number of supplements you need to take.

Essential Nutritionals

In this chapter, we provide specifics about what are known as Infinity[2]'s "Essential Nutritionals," the most effective, most beneficial products available to meet the world's current replenishment needs. These products have been formulated based on peer-reviewed research by a team of the world's leading authorities in the area of health and nutrition. Some people may question why we have chosen to focus on "our" product line. The answer is simple. In writing this book, our commitment is to recommend what is best for health. As we conducted our own search for wellness, we were unable to find products that were formulated based on the principles we knew must be adhered to. The experts concurred that most of the supplements available were not based on research, but were concocted as moneymaking enterprises.

Based on the input from these experts, the Infinity[2] formulations truly address our current nutritional needs. They are unsurpassed in effectiveness because they are made to work with the natural functioning of the body and to ensure delivery at the cellular level.

But, we don't want you to simply take our word for it. Use the information in this section to become educated and to understand how to recognize a good product and to compare the Infinity[2] products with other supplements on the market.

The Core of the Infinity² Essential Nutritionals:
Infinity² Essentials For Life System

The core of the Infinity²'s Essential Nutritionals is the Infinity² Essentials For Life System. All of the daily nutritional requirements necessary to ensure consistent health and vitality are found in one super-powered, easy-to-use regimen: Infinity² Essentials For Life System. This system is the world's first 100% natural, whole food, full spectrum nutritional system that addresses every single aspect of your body's daily nutritional supplementation needs.

The key essential supplementation needs for nutrition on a daily basis are vitamins, minerals, enzymes, flora and antioxidants.

1. Digestive enzymes allow your body to receive maximum nutrition and energy from your food, as well as properly digest fats.

2. Friendly flora strengthen your body's immune system and support your overall health.

3. Antioxidants help protect you from the serious health risks of free radical damage caused by pollution, toxins, and stress.

4. Whole food vitamins are essential to the creation of energy.

5. Amino acid chelated minerals promote stronger bones, healthy hair, skin and nails, help maintain firm muscle tone and assist in the regulation of sugars.

Replenishment Need #1: Enzymes

As discussed in the "Do I Need" chapter, we must replenish our body's enzyme stores because many of the foods we eat are cooked and processed, and, therefore, enzyme-deficient.

Studies prove that eating enzyme-deficient foods causes "digestive leukocytosis" in which the white blood cell count rises, just as it does when the body is sick or has ingested poison. In other words, when you eat cooked food your body must mobilize its immune system to deal with what it sees as a foreign substance.[2]

Thus, eating cooked and processed foods puts tremendous stress on the body, causing us to age prematurely and reducing longevity. Could this be why the average life span is 75 when we should live to be 120?

When enzymes are not present in food, not only is the body overtaxed, but food is often only partially digested. Partially digested food causes additional problems including allergies, lethargy and plaque build-up in the blood vessels.[3]

Initially, the body often reacts to enzyme deficiency with what we call "indigestion." Indigestion manifests itself through uncomfortable and unpleasant symptoms, ranging from burping, heartburn, abdominal pain and bad breath to excess gas, skin problems, diarrhea, constipation and more. But the problem goes beyond minor discomfort. A lack of enzymes interferes with hormone production, inhibits cellular repair, and causes digestive problems to become chronic.[4] Symptoms of indigestion are often treated with preparations that stop digestion, such as antacids like Tums or Rolaids, or acid inhibitors, such as Tagamet, Zantac or Pepcid-AC. This trend is creating major health concerns.

Enzyme Supply Must Be Replenished

Although in today's world it is impractical, almost impossible, to eat a diet of only raw foods, we must replenish our enzyme supply in order to avoid the wide range of "cooked food" diseases. This can be done easily and safely by including an enzyme supplement each time we eat a meal or snack that is cooked or processed. However, keep in mind that not all enzyme supplements are the same.

Pioneering scientist, Dr. Edward Howell conducted much of the enzyme research that has been done, and his findings are chronicled in his book, Enzyme Nutrition. When we began our search for truth, we went to the source that we knew would have the most accurate information. We went to the company founded by Dr. Howell; a company now called National Enzyme Company. In particular, we worked with a chemist who was then vice-president and technical director, Stan Bynum, PhD. The result is a full spectrum of enzymes included as part of the Infinity[2] Essentials For Life System.

Most enzyme formulas on the market, particularly single-plant enzyme products, such as papaya or pineapple enzymes, are not complete. Infinity[2] Essentials For Life System contains a full complex of enzymes so all foods can be broken down into their simplest form. For example, protease initiates the digestion of protein, but breaks it down only to a peptide. Peptides can't be used by the body and can cause more harm than good. Therefore, Infinity[2] Essentials For Life System also includes peptidase in order to break the peptides down to useable amino acids.

Works in All Stages of Digestion

Infinity[2] Essentials For Life System is also unique because it works in all three stages of digestion. Only pure plant enzymes can withstand the changes in temperature and pH levels that occur during the digestive process. Animal enzymes, such as pepsin, don't work in all stages of digestion. Studies also show that animal enzymes may interfere with the body's natural functioning. Infinity[2] Essentials For Life System includes only plant enzymes. For example, rather than the animal-enzyme, pepsin that many formulations include, Infinity[2] Essentials For Life System contains the plant enzyme form (peptidase) instead.

Not just what we eat but what we digest determines our health.

Replenishment Need #2: Friendly Flora

Our second replenishment need stems from the fact that our "friendly flora" have been depleted. A healthy human intestine has about three pounds of these bacteria strains, but recent studies show that most of us have less than half that amount.[5] "Friendly flora" helps rid the body of toxins, aids in digestion and energy production, and perhaps most importantly, protects us from disease. In fact, these bacteria strains are often called "probiotics," meaning "favoring life." (As opposed to "antibiotic," meaning "against life.")

Chemist Stan Bynum, PhD predicts, "Enzyme depletion along with the depletion of friendly flora will combine to bring about the 'Plague of the 21st Century.' Because our helpful bacteria have been destroyed, we no longer have a second line of defense to protect our systems. We are extremely vulnerable to infections that we once believed were a thing of the past."[6]

Indeed, infectious diseases are on the rise. In the first edition of Complete Physique, we cited the 1988 U.S. Surgeon General's Report. At that time, infectious disease was not one of the top 10 causes of death. Does it seem strange that in 1988 infectious disease was so rare that it didn't even make the list, and yet today it is the number six reason people are dying. These diseases are reemerging at a frightening pace.

The Wrong Approach

Ironically, the strategy used to protect us from disease-causing bacteria also puts us at risk. Antibiotics administered to kill harmful bacteria destroy the helpful strains as well. Yet, studies show antibiotic prescriptions are on the rise, particularly for children.[7] Also, half of the 32 billion pounds of antibiotics produced are given to animals to cure infections and for faster growth. Therefore, we very likely take in antibiotics when we eat meat, milk or other animal products.

Laxatives, birth control pills, strong antibacterial herbs, frequent fasting, eating disorders, and chlorine and fluoride in water also deplete flora. In addition, carbonated drinks, coffee and alcohol, poor diets, even aging, stress, and emotional upsets destroy the bacteria we need for health.[8]

What the Expert Says

To address this need, we drew on the expertise of Dr. Khem Shahani, the world's leading probiotic expert, from the University of Nebraska. Dr. Shahani has done more research and published more peer-reviewed journal articles on probiotics than any other individual.

Many companies understand the importance of friendly flora, but they generally produce probiotic products that contain only one species or one type of bacteria. However, according to research by Dr. Shahani and others, single species of bacteria are not enough to be effective. A probiotic formulation must include twelve species of bacteria. Plus, these strains must be stabilized. A "stabilized" strain is resilient enough to withstand the conditions encountered during digestion.

Infinity² Essentials for Life System contains twelve exceptionally superior probiotic species. The acidophilus included in Infinity² Essentials for Life System is particularly hearty. This strain, called Lactobacillus Acidophilus was developed and stabilized according to a patented process researched by Dr. Shahani.

Replenishment Need #3: Antioxidants

The third reason most people need replenishment is caused by our environment. Billions of pounds of environmental toxins are dumped into our air, our water and our soil every year. Every individual living in an industrialized nation is at risk, even if he or she lives in a rural area. With every breath, every glass of water, every bite of food, we take in highly reactive molecules called "free radicals."

Free radicals are actually oxygen molecules that are missing an electron. They result from smog, chemicals, paint and household cleaners; and from electronic devices, including televisions and computers. These molecules are like "loose cannons," bombarding every cell of our body, and robbing the electrons they need from paired molecules, thus, creating more free radicals. It has been estimated that every cell of our body takes over 10,000 "hits" a day.[9]

Free Radicals Result in Disease

These free radical "hits" weaken the cell walls, and the damage they cause has been linked to over 85 diseases, including heart disease, cancer, arthritis, cataracts and emphysema. Free radicals also cause joint pain, eye strain, shortness of breath, and signs that are normally associated with aging, such as dry skin, wrinkles and age spots.

In effect, free radicals cause the body to "oxidize," much like a tin can will oxidize as it ages. In order to defuse these damaging molecules and stop the process of oxidation, our bodies need nutrients called antioxidants.

Stop the Oxidation

Antioxidants are nutrients that intercept the oxidation process and "put the brake on chain reactions to stop the re-creation of numerous other oxidants [free radicals]."[10] An antioxidant also "repairs damage caused by the oxidants that don't get intercepted."[11] In recent years, much has been published concerning the importance of antioxidant nutrients. However, antioxidants vary in quality and effectiveness. For several years, researchers have proclaimed the benefits of vitamins A, C, E and the mineral selenium. These nutrients do help offset the effects of free radicals. However, in recent years, another class of nutrients called proanthocyanidins has been proven to be as much as twenty times more effective than vitamin C and fifty times more effective than vitamin E.

Working with the experts, we determined that the Infinity² Essentials For Life System must include proanthocyanidins from Maritime Pine Bark Extract, the best proanthocyanidin source. It provides the best possible antioxidant protection. Also, specific "macerating," enzymes were included in Infinity² Essentials For Life System to further boost the active constituents of the pine bark, making this formulation extremely potent.

Assist the Body's Free Radical Fighting Forces

Even more important than supplying powerful antioxidant ingredients, unlike any other antioxidant supplement, Infinity² Essentials For Life System helps the body become a better free radical fighter. That means, Infinity² Essentials For Life System is the only supplement that doesn't encourage the body to become dependent on a supplemental antioxidant. Let us explain. As powerful as proanthocyanidins are, they do not match the effectiveness of the body's own antioxidant, superoxide dismutase (SOD). However, SOD cannot be absorbed if taken as a supplement. Instead, based on research conducted by Dr. Harvey Ashmead, founder of Albion Laboratories and holder of over 50 international patents, we have included exclusive, patented SOD Precursors™, or what might be called SOD "building blocks." Our SOD Precursors supply the body with what it needs to make SOD. That means you won't continually need to increase your dosage of Infinity² Essentials For Life System, as is the case with most free radical fighting products. Infinity² Essentials For Life System provides powerful protection by reinforcing your own free radical fighting forces.

We took still another important matter into consideration. When the interaction between an antioxidant and a free radical takes place, toxic residue is created. Most antioxidant formulators provide no way to rid the body of this toxic debris. In fact, if you have ever taken an antioxidant, such as a powerful Pycnogenol, you may have noticed some initial relief of certain symptoms; but after a short time of being on the product, you may have found the benefits ceased, or that you needed to take more product to get the same results. Most likely, you were experiencing a setback because of an increase in toxic waste created by the antioxidant/free radical interaction. Infinity² Essentials For Life System includes a tripeptide and an enzyme to effectively "clean up" the waste.

Replenishment Need #4: Whole Food Vitamins

Study after study shows that it is becoming more difficult to get the vitamins and minerals the body needs from our foods. Because of soil depletion, ozone layer depletion, pesticides and over-processing, our foods are often left devoid of these vital nutrients. If you have any doubt, we suggest you go to your local library and look up the reports from your national department of agriculture to see how each year foods become more depleted of enzymes, vitamins and minerals.

As pointed out in the "Do I Need" chapter, even a minor nutrient deficiency can begin to erode our health, so supplying supplemental vitamins is crucial. However, not just any vitamin will do.

Vitamins Must Be Familiar to the Body

It's vital that supplemental vitamins and minerals are in a form that the body can easily and completely use. To be assimilated in the body, vitamins must be whole food complexes. Whole food complexes are foods with only the water and fiber removed. These vitamins are natural and familiar to the body. On the other hand, synthetic, fractionated vitamins are only a portion or an imitation of the whole food complex, and are not readily useable in the body

To absorb and utilize a fractionated vitamin, the body must complete the nutrient complex by drawing the missing elements from bodily tissues and bones, especially the collagen tissue in the case of vitamin C. Thus, taking a fractionated vitamin can actually create a vitamin deficiency.

Another example is vitamin E. Whole food vitamin E strengthens the bones. However, large doses of alpha tocopherol, a fractionated form of vitamin E, actually cause bone tissue to release vitamins and minerals in order to compensate. This causes the loss of calcium and other nutrients from the bone, contributing to eventual deterioration and disease. Doesn't it defeat the purpose of taking a supplement if that supplement robs from the body, rather than giving the body what it needs?

The unfortunate results of taking fractionated vitamins recently made headlines. Doctors found that taking beta carotene (a fraction of vitamin A) actually increases the risk of cancer, while eating the whole foods that contain beta carotene, such as broccoli and cabbage, significantly reduces that risk. Recent research even ties synthetic vitamins to heart disease.

Whole Food Vitamin C

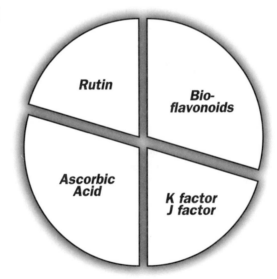

Look for Whole Food Vitamins

In contrast, natural, whole food complexes don't interfere with the body's normal biochemical processes. Instead, they supply the nutrients each cell can use for recuperation and function. When selecting a vitamin supplement, read the label and look for food names listed as the vitamin sources. For example, avoid products that list "ascorbic acid" as the source for vitamin C. There is no such thing as an ascorbic acid plant! Instead, select products that list "acerola cherries," or another ingredient you recognize as a food.

Whole food vitamins don't supply an artificial burst of energy that quickly goes away. Instead, they provide a constant health-promoting energy source that you can depend on throughout the day. To meet the need for a multi-vitamin supplement, our formulation team included only whole food vitamins in Infinity² Essentials For Life System.

Replenishment Need #5: Amino Acid Chelated Minerals

Infinity² has always felt that the major source of minerals should be a healthy diet. However, two factors have influenced our Formulation Team to include additional minerals in the Infinity² Essentials For Life. These factors are:

1. Studies performed at Rutgers University by a research group headed by Dr. Firman E. Bear have revealed an alarming decline in the mineral content of commercially grown foods. In these studies, samples of a variety of basic food crops from different regions of the U.S. were obtained and analyzed and the values recorded. This procedure was repeated each year using samples of the same foods obtained from the same regions until ten years of annual sampling had been performed. In almost every case, the nutrient mineral content values were lower each year than that of the previous year. These Rutgers University studies have been confirmed by similar results from a research group at the University of Missouri, headed by Dr. William Albrecht. Clearly, these results warn us that the foods that we have relied upon for our nutrient minerals are no longer dependable sources.

2. Even though we advocate a diet consisting of whole, fresh and raw foods as a first principle of health, we are aware that most people in our society have very busy and pressure-packed lifestyles making it very difficult to maintain a completely healthy food intake.

For these two very compelling reasons, we are convinced that a complete, high-potency supplemental intake of all the nutrient minerals is a part of the core nutritional supplementation program embodied in the Infinity² Nutritionals.

Minerals Selected

Considerable confusion seems to exist in the dietary supplement industry on the subject of minerals as nutrients. In some cases, as with "colloidal minerals," it is assumed that all minerals have nutritional value. In fact, the minerals that are considered to be nutrients are strictly defined by six criteria:

1. Presence in healthy tissue of all living things.

2. Fairly constant concentration from one animal species to the next.

3. Withdrawal from the body induces the same abnormalities, regardless of species studied.

4. Re-introduction reduces or prevents these abnormalities.

5. The abnormalities are always accompanied by specific biochemical changes, such as reduction in activity of a specific enzyme.

6. The biochemical changes can be prevented or cured when the deficiency is prevented or cured.

There are twenty-one minerals that meet these criteria. They are calcium, phosphorous, magnesium, sodium, potassium, chloride, iron, zinc, copper, selenium, chromium, iodine, manganese, molybdenum, fluoride, nickel, silicon, vanadium, arsenic, boron, and cobalt. Of these, there are not known to be deficiencies in humans of phosphorous, sodium, chloride, nickel, silicon or arsenic. Potassium, while sometimes deficient in certain diseases, is not one of the minerals that are depleted from commercially grown foods (because it is added to commercial fertilizers). Iodine is commonly added to foods, and its deficiency has become rare. Cobalt is only an essential nutrient in humans as vitamin B-12. Supplementation with fluoride is not considered prudent because its level of requirement is too close to the level at which toxicity occurs. This leaves calcium, magnesium, iron, zinc, copper, selenium, chromium, manganese, molybdenum, vanadium and boron as the appropriate ingredients of a complete mineral supplement, and these are the mineral ingredients of in the Infinity² Essentials For Life System.

Sources of Minerals

The quality of a source of minerals as a human dietary supplement is defined by two parameters:

1. Lack of toxicity, meaning that high doses of the mineral can be ingested without adversely affecting human health;

2. Bioavailability, meaning that once the supplement is ingested, its ingredients can actually be shown to reach the environment of the cell and produce benefit in terms of healthy function.

With respect to both of these parameters, the amino acid chelate minerals produced by Albion Laboratories of Clearfield, Utah, have (by far) the best record of research and performance. For example, studies conducted at the University of Nebraska by Dr. R. P. Heaney showed that the bioavailability of calcium given as the amino acid chelate is approximately three times that of most other sources of supplemental calcium. Numerous studies on toxic effects of various levels of supplemental minerals have revealed that the highest level of safety is obtained by supplementing minerals in the amino acid chelate form. For these reasons, only amino acid chelated minerals are utilized in the Infinity² Essentials For Life System. Fortunately, the Infinity² formulation team includes members of the scientific staff of Albion Laboratories, whose input was critical to the formulation of the unique mineral blend included in the Infinity² Essentials For Life System.

Replenishment Need #6: Lipase and Chromium for fats and sugars

In our research, we discovered that an additional supplementation need exists because the vast majority of the population consumes unhealthy amounts of sugar and enzyme-deficient fat. Consider these facts:

1. Most of the fat we consume is cooked and, thus, devoid of enzymes.

2. Often the low-fat foods we eat in order to trim fat from our diets are extremely high in sugar and preservatives.

3. Even if we are now restricting fat and sugar, we may have health problems because of over-consumption of fat and sugar in the past.

4. Fats and sugars are often "hidden" in the prepared "convenience" foods we eat.

Excess fat leads to obesity and a myriad of associated health concerns. Obesity puts the body's organs through extreme stress, causing a wide range of degenerative diseases and shortening the life span. Over 75 million people in the United States could be considered obese[12]. The number of overweight Americans actually rose from 26 percent in 1980 to 34 percent in 1991[13], and is still rising. The 1994 NHANES report recorded 32.6 percent of the population as moderately overweight, and 22.3 percent as severely overweight[14]. In 1999, a report in the New England Journal of Medicine reported that the risk of death increases throughout the range of moderate and severe overweight for both mean and women and in all age groups.[15] However, even people who don't have excess stored fat, often have undigested fat in the bloodstream, which can lead to heart disease and atherosclerosis, the leading causes of death today.

Fat Is Not the Problem

Many people think the answer is to severely reduce fat intake. Yet, fat itself is not the problem. Twenty percent of a person's diet should be from fats to promote proper organ function and healthy hair and skin. Fat is also the best source of energy. The problem is that most of the fat we eat is from poor sources, isn't raw and cannot be readily digested. The enzyme lipase is necessary to break fat down so it can be used for energy. Without lipase, fat is stored or it is only partially broken down, meaning it can then circulate in the bloodstream and cling to the walls of the arteries. Lipase is not present in most diets. Therefore, supplementing with this important enzyme is vital to health.

Eating too much sugar creates mood swings, cravings and headaches and can lead to hypoglycemic or diabetic tendencies. Sugar can interfere with consistent production of insulin, the hormone that the body secretes to help control hunger, and regulate energy, fat burning and muscle building. Insulin surges can cause people to eat 60 to 70 percent more at the following meal. Although low in calories, sugar can make you store body fat and increase blood triglyceride levels[16]. (Hence, buyer beware when it comes to "fat-free" – but high-sugar – cookies, cakes and other snacks!)

Recent research[16] has shown that eating a diet high in simple sugars causes the liver to produce more triglycerides, which raises blood triglycerides (a risk factor for heart disease). This same research has shown a possible link between increased triglycerides and diabetes[16].

Chromium — Essential for Insulin Function

These problems are compounded because an estimated 90 percent of Americans fail to meet the daily requirements for the mineral chromium[17]. Chromium insures that insulin works efficiently and plays an essential role in carbohydrate and fat metabolism[18]. Chromium deficiency causes fatigue, leads to excess fat production, and is a major contributor to heart disease and diabetes. This deficiency, coupled with the abuse of fat and sugars, can be linked to the lack of energy, mood swings and obesity that so many people experience.

Much has been publicized about chromium, but the chromium that is often promoted is not in the best form. Chromium picolinate, which is chromium bound to picolinic acid, has been shown to cause liver toxicity and has also been linked to cancer[19]. Once again, we relied on a team of experts as we formulated Infinity[2] Essentials For Life to address this common health concern. As a result extra lipase and a patented form of chromium have been added to the Infinity[2] Essentials For Life System.

Prior to Infinity[2] Essentials for Life System it took a minimum of six separate nutritional products to meet all these needs. The Infinity[2] Essentials For Life System takes care of all five of theses nutritional requirements in one easy and convenient system. And, at the heart of Infinity[2]'s all natural Essentials For Life System is CAeDS®, an exclusive nutrient delivery system that guarantees maximum effectiveness. CAeDS (Chelate Activated Enzyme Delivery System) is composed of the exact enzymes and co-factors needed to facilitate complete absorption of all the natural ingredients. When combined with the full range of minerals, enzymes and flora; the most complete whole food vitamins and powerful antioxidants available; plus a superior fat digester and sugar regulator, it makes the Infinity[2] Essentials For Life System the most powerful nutritional system on the planet.

The Other Infinity[2] Essential Nutritionals

For many people, the Infinity[2] Essentials For Life System will meet all of their daily nutritional supplement requirements. However, some people may have extra needs due to specific health conditions, environmental factors or other circumstances in their life. For these individuals we recommend they include one of the individual Infinity[2] Essential Nutritionals to supply those extra needs.

Digest-a-Meal™

Enzymes are essential for health. They are the literal "life force" of every bodily function. Without these powerful bio-chemical catalysts, the body cannot function optimally, and life itself cannot continue. Although digestive enzymes occur naturally in our foods, they are destroyed by commercial growing, cooking and processing methods. Carbonated drinks, strenuous exercise, environmental factors, and stress further deplete our enzyme stores. Digest-a-Meal replenishes vital digestive enzymes so that metabolic enzymes can be spared for other life-generating functions. Digest-a-Meal is vital to the health of virtually every individual.

- Supplies complete enzyme complexes so that all foods are broken down to their most useable form.

- Takes the burden of digestion off the body, allowing other functions to proceed unimpaired.

- Assures that nutrients from food or nutritional supplements are absorbed by the body.

- Delivers nutrients on the cellular level.

- Includes an exclusive system which ensures enzyme activity in all stages of digestion.

- Promotes proper digestion, which enhances health, increases energy levels and promotes longevity.

Digest-a-Meal, with its pure plant enzymes, assured enzyme activity and exclusive delivery system, stands alone as the ultimate enzyme formula. Digest-a-Meal also includes a special combination of minerals that are a part of Infinity²'s Chelate Activated Enzyme Delivery System (CAᵉDS™), which ensures that the enzymes in Digest-a-Meal are absorbed and utilized.

What the Expert Says

Stan Bynum, PhD says, "I have formulated hundreds of enzyme products for various companies. Infinity²'s Digest-a-Meal surpasses them all. No other formulation ensures complete digestion. No other formulation contains a system, which assures optimum enzyme functioning, without "leeching" anything from the body. Compared to the other enzyme products available, I know Digest-a-Meal is far superior. For digestive health, I will take no other enzyme supplement, but Digest-a-Meal."

When the world's leading authority in enzyme nutrition — a man who has been involved in the formulation process with over 200 companies as they created their enzyme supplements — selects Digest-a-Meal as the only enzyme supplement for his own and his family's health, it's obvious that Digest-a-Meal is clearly superior. The results have been superior, as well, for individuals in all walks of life.

What Others Say About Digest-a-Meal

Theresa Gregory, from Mount Vernon, Ohio, says, "For the last twenty years, I've had digestive problems. After years of medical testing with no real answer, I found Digest-a-Meal to be the missing link. I feel better at age forty-two than I did at twenty-two."

Jim McKellar, of Guelph, Ontario, Canada, says, "I have suffered from Crohn's Disease, arthritis, allergies and indigestion for over 15 years. I had part of my intestinal tract removed in 1988 and was hospitalized twice in 1995 with severe pain and diarrhea. I began taking Digest-a-Meal, and within a few days, I had no more pain or diarrhea. Also, my arthritis, allergies and indigestion have disappeared. Remarkable."

Mark Bramblett, of Roanoke, Virginia, says, "I was diagnosed with serious acid reflux. I even had to sleep in a tilted bed because the acid would come up into my mouth at night and cause sores. Within two weeks of taking Digest-a-Meal, I was able to throw my medication and my Tums away."

Take Digest-a-Meal during any meal or snack that includes cooked or processed foods. This relieves the body of the stressful burden of digestion and promotes overall health. Fill out the questionnaire at the end of this chapter to determine the dosage of Digest-a-Meal you currently need and to identify lifestyle factors that you can change so you can decrease that dosage.

Total Flora Support™

Having a sufficient amount of "friendly flora," or "good" bacteria, in your intestines is the key to boosting the immune system. These bacteria are destroyed by such common factors as carbonated drinks, laxatives, birth control pills, coffee, alcohol, aging, stress and antibiotics (even antibiotics found in the meat we eat).

Friendly bacteria strains can suppress harmful bacteria, aid in digestion and elimination, improve absorption of minerals, and reduce toxins in the bloodstream. Infinity²'s formulation has not one but twelve strains of these "good-guy" bacteria. These twelve strains are selected and manufactured according to the proprietary processes developed by Dr. Khem Shahani, the world's leading expert in the area of friendly bacteria.

- Acts as the body's "second immune system".

- Proven to improve digestion and elimination.

- Wards off disease by suppressing harmful bacteria.

- Produces enzymes, which are essential to proper intestinal function.

- Reduces blood fat and cholesterol levels.

Even if another supplement were to combine these twelve powerful species, our formulation would still be a step ahead. Fructooligosacharrides (FOS), which are basically food for the bacteria, have been added to help them grow and flourish more rapidly, thus increasing their potency. In addition, our patented Chelate Activated Enzyme Delivery System (CA^{e}DS) has also been included to aid in the assimilation and delivery of these twelve important strains. This careful formulation makes Total Flora Support the most useful, health-promoting bacteria supplement available. Dr. Shahani was so impressed with this particular formula and with the philosophy behind the Infinity^2 formulations that he has joined with other health authorities as a member of the Infinity^2 Product Formulation Team, and was instrumental in developing Total Flora Support.

What the Experts Say...

Dr. Shahani says, "Total Flora Support brings together important results of scientific and biotechnological research that I have been involved in for almost 40 years. I have been impressed with Infinity^2's commitment to provide the very best flora product available."

Dr. Kent A. Guisinger, D.O., from Lancaster, Ohio, has seen amazing results using this formula in his practice. He says, "Total Flora Support has helped a great deal in patients with candidiasis, chronic fatigue syndrome, diverticulitis, constipation, ulcerative colitis and obesity."

It is best to take Total Flora Support with meals in order to encourage the rapid implantation and growth of these powerful bacteria strains. Complete the "How Much Do I Need" questionnaire to determine how many capsules you should take. You will be able to reduce that amount as you make the lifestyle changes indicated on the questionnaire.

Life Force Super Antioxidant™

Antioxidants work in the body to defuse highly reactive molecules called "free radicals." Free radicals – the result of environmental toxins, stress, and overexercise – constantly bombard the body's cells, causing cell walls to weaken and allowing disease and degeneration to set in.

Since free radical damage has been linked to over 85 diseases, the need for a powerful antioxidant has never been grater. Only Life Force Super Antioxidant wages a complete attack, supplying the most potent ingredients, boosting the body's ability to fight free radicals, and ensuring that the waste products from the free radical/antioxidant interaction are taken care of.

- Supplies a unique combination of the most potent antioxidant ingredients available – Maritime Pine Bark Extract and Grape Seed Extract

- Includes "macerating enzymes" which are proven to increase the potency of Grape Seed Extract.

- Exclusive SOD Precursor System uses a mineral complex to supply the "building blocks" so the body can make its own powerful antioxidant (SOD) thus providing the finest antioxidant protection without having to rely solely on antioxidant supplement.

- Ensures that waste products from the antioxidant/free radical interaction are not left to build up and cause damage in the body.

- Offers the most complete, most effective antioxidant protection available.

Because Life Force Super Antioxidant supplies the most powerful free-radical fighting ingredients, helps the body become a better free radical fighter, and takes care of the toxic waste, you can see why we call it a "wholistic" formulation. It is the first and only wholistic formulation on the market. This amazing, complete antioxidant also includes our Chelate Activated Enzyme Delivery System (CA^{e}DS).

"Super" Results

Life Force Super Antioxidant has proven to be highly effective for a wide range of conditions. For example, we have heard testimonials that children with hyperactivity or bed-wetting tendencies have been helped with Life Force Super Antioxidant. This amazing antioxidant has helped to nutritionally support cancer patients and HIV patients.

One user, Frances Aust, says, "I am 67 years old and was diagnosed with macular degeneration. With limited sight in my right eye, I was not pleased to learn my left eye would likely follow suit. I began taking Life Force Super Antioxidant and two weeks later I had better test results and I saw improvement in both eyes. I give full credit for my amazing recovery to Life Force Super Antioxidant."

What Doctors Say about Life Force Super Antioxidant

David M. Creech, M.D. FACS says, "after the orthopedic procedure to reconstruct my anterior cruciate ligament (ACL) of my knee, I began the post-surgical protocol recommended by Infinity^2. My personal experience was exceptionally gratifying. The swelling in my knee diminished rapidly....Due to my personal positive experience with Infinity^2 antioxidants, I began to use the post-surgery protocol of Life Force and Cytolyse for my own patients recuperating from facial cosmetic surgery and liposuction."

For maximum antioxidant protection and to increase your body's ability to fight free radicals, use Life Force Super Antioxidant. To determine your specific requirements, refer to the "How Much Do I Need" questionnaire at the end of this chapter.

Insure Plus™

Even balanced diets are dangerously lacking in essential
nutrients. Over 95 percent of the North American population
are deficient in some nutrient. Supplementation is crucial,
yet all multi-vitamin supplements are not created equal.
Insure Plus is the only formulation that completely obeys the
laws of nature – supplying the finest ingredients: whole food
vitamins, patented chelated minerals, and an exclusive delivery system.

Because we heeded natural laws when formulating
Insure Plus, this one-of-a-kind supplement provides the
body with the richest benefits possible for every individual –
children, teens and adults.

- Your best nutritional "insurance policy," supplying the nutrients
  missing in the foods we eat.

- Provides an excellent source of B complex vitamins, which are
  essential for energy and blood cell health.

- Includes a unique patented delivery system that guarantees delivery of
  nutrients to the site where they are needed.

- Provides only whole food vitamin complexes, the only vitamin form that
  will truly support proper tissue repair and regeneration.

- Helps balance and nourish the body, making it more resistant to
  disease and degeneration.

In addition to traditional vitamins, Insure Plus contains a source of essential fatty
acids. Essential fatty acids are necessary for maintaining immune system function,
rebuilding and producing new cells, and for maintaining proper brain and nervous-
system function.

Like a nutritional insurance policy, Insure Plus is formulated to give you all the
vitamins your body needs. Plus, each of the food sources was painstakingly
researched to identify any naturally occurring enzymes, minerals and botanical constituents that may have been lost in the formulation process. Those elements were
then added back in Insure Plus. This formulation also has our Chelate Activated
Enzyme Delivery System (CAᵉDS) to deliver the nutrients directly to the site where
they are needed. This powerful formulation is indeed the most complete nutritional
"insurance" available.

What Others say about Insure Plus

Carl Ross from Galion, Ohio, says, "My wife, Betty, and I used to take other supplements, but evidently our bodies weren't absorbing them...Even though I was taking vitamins and minerals, I suffered from low back and leg pain when I stood for any
time at all. When we started taking the Infinity² products, I could tell that the ingredi-

ents in Insure Plus were being absorbed because three weeks into the Infinity² program, my back and leg pain was reduced by 90 percent. We both use all the Nutritionals and have really noticed a difference."

The best testimonial for this one-of-a-kind product will be your own. Like thousands of others, you may very well notice a difference almost immediately, since with Insure Plus, you will be getting the very best a multi-vitamin and mineral supplement can provide. Refer to the questionnaire to determine how many capsules you need to take daily.

Chelated Mineral Complex™

Mineral deficiencies are common and can lead to problems ranging from lowered immunity and a sluggish metabolism to anemia and cancer. Most of us have very busy and pressure-packed lifestyles that make it very difficult to maintain a completely healthy food intake and, as a result, do not obtain adequate amounts of minerals from our diet. Cooking and processing our foods robs the food of its essential nutrients. In addition, studies have revealed an alarming decline in the mineral content of commercially grown food, making it even more difficult to obtain the amount of nutrients required for optimum health.

Inadequate mineral nutrition has been associated with a variety of human diseases, including anemia, high blood pressure, diabetes, cancer, tooth decay, and osteoporosis. Thus proper dietary intake of essential minerals is necessary for optimal health, energy, vitality, and physical performance. Unfortunately, most people do not obtain enough nutrient minerals to sustain optimum health, making supplementation of minerals crucial.

Infinity² Chelated Mineral Complex is a proprietary blend of eleven nutrient minerals in a unique balance, specifically formulated to replenish the common mineral deficiencies in the current human dietary pattern of the developed countries of the world. All of the minerals in this formula are supplied as Albion Amino Acid Chelates, the best absorbed, best tolerated and most bioavailable mineral form. Amino Acid Chelated minerals are absorbed as amino acids rather than minerals, so they have the highest absorption rate possible allowing for increased utilization by the body. In addition to using the most bioavailable minerals, Infinity² Chelated Mineral Complex also includes a specially designed CAᵉDS system which guards the minerals from deactivation and assures cellular delivery. With more of the mineral available in the system, the body will have adequate supplies to build new tissues, activate enzymes, and regulate hormones.

The nutrients in Infinity²'s Chelated Mineral Complex help:

- Prevent "leaching" of minerals from the skeletal structures of the body.

- Activate the enzyme systems of the body for better digestion, metabolism, and overall body function.

- Normalize immune function and increase resistance to disease.

- Improve function and appearance of skin.

- Produce healthy blood cells.

- Maintain healthy hair and nails.

To get the optimum balance of minerals, use Infinity²'s Chelated Mineral Complex. To determine your specific requirements, refer to the "How Much Do I Need" questionnaire at the end of this chapter.

Lipo-chromizyme™

What started as a healthy concern for trimming fat has resulted in a society which views dietary fat as an insipid monster. Fat is not bad. It is essential for healthy skin and hair and is a major component in the proper functioning of every bodily system. Without fat, precious energy stores are depleted and metabolism slows to an unhealthy crawl. The problem isn't the fat itself; it's undigested fat.

To avoid fats, many individuals turn to "fat-free" packaged meals, which are often high in sugar and salt. The all-too-common over-consumption of sugar can result in mood swings, food cravings, headaches and overeating at the next meal, as well as hypoglycemic or diabetic tendencies.

Lipo-chromizyme (Chrome ZME™ in Canada) is a one-of-a-kind supplement that effectively addresses the problems caused by dietary fats and refined sugars. First, this unique product includes the fat digesting enzyme, lipase. Many products on the market claim to be "fat blockers" or "fat burners." These products actually interfere with fat digestion and block the fat from doing its job of supplying energy. By supplying the enzyme lipase, Lipo-chromizyme ensures that fat is digested and broken down for energy production.

Also unique to this formulation is the patented amino acid chelate, Chromium Chelavite™, a highly bioavailable form of chromium. And, like the other Infinity² products, Lipo-chromizyme has our exclusive delivery system.

- Increases energy by making fat available for use in the system.

- Not a fat burner or blocker, but a fat digester that allows the body to use fat stores.

- Includes a patented chromium source, proven to support healthy insulin function, minimize mood swings, level out sugar highs and lows, and reduce food cravings.

- Increases the body's ability to make lean muscle and burn fat while exercising.

- Helps break down undigested fats, which, if circulating in the bloodstream, may lead to arteriosclerosis and heart disease.

Lipo-chromizyme is the best natural supplement for addressing the problems associated with dietary fats and sugars, and is unequaled in helping to reduce fat stores, retain lean muscle, enhance energy and support healthy insulin function.

Gea Johnson, United States Power Lifting Team and Heptathlete Contender 2000 Olympics says, "Thanks to Lipo-chromizyme, I have more energy, balance and a lower body fat percentage because I am consistently burning fat for fuel rather than just storing it."

What the Doctor Orders

A Gilbert, Arizona, chiropractor says, "I have seen significant results using Lipo-chromizyme with my patients, and I have verified those results with traditional blood tests. Lipo-chromizyme helps the body metabolize fat for increased energy and overall improved bodily function. I recommend Lipo-chromizyme to anyone trying to reduce body fat or stabilize conditions of blood sugar imbalance."

For best results, take one to two Lipo-chromizyme capsules with each meal, particularly meals high in enzyme-deficient fat or sugar. Also, take between meals to help control cravings and keep energy and mood levels constant. You may also want to take two Lipo-chromizyme capsules before workouts to maintain fat burning while exercising. Again, use the "How Much Do I Need?" questionnaire below to determine how much Lipo-chromizyme is appropriate for you.

The supplements discussed in this chapter are the Infinity²'s "Nutritionals," the foundational supplements that virtually every individual needs. Use the questionnaire that follows to determine your recommended dosages and to identify lifestyle changes that will help you eventually reduce the number of supplements you need to take for health.

How Much Do I Need? Questionnaire

Digest-a-Meal

	No	Sometimes	Often
Lifestyle Choices			
Do you eat cooked and/or processed food?	0	1	2
Do you eat rapidly, without chewing thoroughly?	0	1	2
Do you eat until you feel full?	0	1	2
Do you drink carbonated beverages?	0	1	2
Do you drink coffee or tea?	0	1	2
Do you drink alcoholic beverages?	0	1	2
Symptoms			
Do you experience bloating?	0	1	2
Do you feel too full after eating?	0	1	2
Do you feel sleepy or have low energy after eating?	0	1	2
Do you have any uncomfortable or adverse reactions after eating?	0	1	2
Do you feel a need to eliminate soon after eating?	0	1	2
Do you have diarrhea after eating?	0	1	2
Do you have difficulty breathing after eating?	0	1	2
Does your food pass through undigested?	0	1	2
Do you get indigestion after eating?	0	1	2

Total _____

Total	Recommended Dosage
0 - 6	Essentials For Life only
7 - 18	1 capsule with each meal, in addition to Essentials For Life
19 - 25	2 capsules with each meal, in addition to Essentials For Life
26 - 30	3 capsules with each meal, in addition to Essentials For Life

Total Flora Support

	No	Sometimes	Often
Lifestyle Choices			
Do you use antibiotics?	0	1	2
Do you eat commercially raised meat?	0	1	2
Do you consume commercially produced dairy products?	0	1	2
Do you drink non-filtered water?	0	1	2
Do you drink chlorinated water?	0	1	2
Do you drink carbonated beverages?	0	1	2
Do you drink coffee or tea?	0	1	2
Do you drink alcoholic beverages?	0	1	2
Have you undergone surgery within the last 90 days?	0	1	2
Have you done any foreign travel within the last 90 days?	0	1	2
Symptoms			
Do you get colds and the flu?	0	1	2
Do you have persistent diarrhea?	0	1	2
Do you get sick often?	0	1	2
Do you have frequent cold sores?	0	1	2
Do you have a history of food poisoning?	0	1	2
Do you have persistent flatulence or gas?	0	1	2
Do you have bad breath?	0	1	2

Total _____

Total	Recommended Dosage
0 - 7	Essentials For Life Only
8 - 13	1 capsule with each meal in addition to Essentials For Life
14 - 34	2 capsules with each meal in addition to Essentials For Life

Life Force Super Antioxidant

	No	Sometimes	Often
Lifestyle Choices			
Do you live or work where there is air pollution?	0	1	2
Do you work on a computer?	0	1	2
Do you use TVs and/or microwave ovens?	0	1	2
Do you exercise excessively?	0	1	2
Do you consume hydrogenated fats?	0	1	2
Do you drink fluoridated water?	0	1	2
Do you avoid cruciferous vegetables (e.g., cauliflower, brussel sprouts, asparagus)?	0	1	2
Do you have stress in your life?	0	1	2
Do you avoid red fruits or vegetables (e.g., tomatoes, cranberries, cherries)?	0	1	2
Do you smoke or are you exposed to secondhand smoke or smog?	0	1	2
Symptoms			
Do you have age spots?	0	1	2
Do you have hemorrhoids?	0	1	2
Do you get bloody noses?	0	1	2
Do you bruise easily or have varicose veins?	0	1	2
Do you have deteriorating eyesight?	0	1	2
Do you experience hyperactivity or excessive nervousness?	0	1	2
Do you have bleeding gums?	0	1	2
Do you have excessive wrinkling of the skin/premature aging?	0	1	2
Do you have stiff joints?	0	1	2

Total _____

Total	Recommended Dosage
0 – 7	Essentials For Life Only
8 – 12	1 capsule morning and night, in addition to Essentials For Life
13 - 17	2 capsules morning and night, in addition to Essentials For Life
18 – 30	3 capsules morning and night, in addition to Essentials For Life
31 – 38	4 capsules morning and night, in addition to Essentials For Life

Note: Double the above dosage of Life Force Super Antioxidant during the first two weeks of use.

Insure Plus

	No	Sometimes	Often
Lifestyle Choices			
Do you eat less than four servings of grain each day?	0	1	2
Do you eat less than three servings of fresh fruit each day?	0	1	2
Do you eat less than two servings of fresh, dark-colored vegetables each day?	0	1	2
Do you eat less than two servings of dairy products each day?	0	1	2
Do you eat food that is not organically grown?	0	1	2
Symptoms			
Do you have persistent leg cramps?	0	1	2
Do you have poor stamina?	0	1	2
Do you have excessive hair loss?	0	1	2
Do you have trouble sleeping?	0	1	2
Do your muscles feel weak after performing usual daily activities?	0	1	2
Do you have a craving for alcohol?	0	1	2
Do you have a small appetite?	0	1	2
Do you have an excessive appetite?	0	1	2
Do you feel nervous or are you unable to concentrate?	0	1	2

Total _____

Total	**Recommended Dosage**
0 – 12	none, Essentials For Life Only
12 – 25	1 capsule with each meal, in addition to Essentials For Life
25 – 28	2 capsules with each meal, in addition to Essentials For Life

Chelated Mineral Complex

	No	Sometimes	Often
Lifestyle Choices			
Do you eat less than four servings of grain each day? 0		1	2
Do you eat less than two servings of fresh, dark-colored vegetables each day? 0		1	2
Do you eat less than two servings of dairy products each day? 0		1	2
Do you eat food that is not organically grown? 0		1	2
Do you exercise three or more days per week? 0		1	2
Symptoms			
Do you have persistent leg cramps? 0		1	2
Do you have poor stamina? 0		1	2
Do you have graying of hair? 0		1	2
Do you have excessive hair loss? 0		1	2
Do you have trouble sleeping? 0		1	2
Do your muscles feel weak after performing usual daily activities? 0		1	2
Do you have a craving for alcohol? 0		1	2
Do you feel nervous or are you unable to concentrate? 0		1	2

Total _____

Total	Recommended Dosage
0 – 12	none, Essentials For Life Only
12 – 20	1 capsule with each meal, in addition to Essentials For Life
20 – 26	2 capsules with each meal, in addition to Essentials For Life

Lipo-chromizyme

	No	Sometimes	Often
Lifestyle Choices			
Do you avoid exercise?.	0	1	2
Do you eat fatty foods?	0	1	2
Do you eat white bread?	0	1	2
Do you eat candy or sweets?.	0	1	2
Do you drink sweet drinks?.	0	1	2
Do you have stress in your life?	0	1	2
Symptoms			
Do you experience mood swings?	0	1	2
Do you experience nervousness or shakiness?	0	1	2
Do you have a craving for sweets or sugars?	0	1	2
Do you experience weakness or faintness between meals?.	0	1	2
Are you unable to gain weight or lose unwanted fat?.	0	1	2
Do you experience excessive fatigue during workouts?	0	1	2
Do you feel you have unstable blood sugar levels?.	0	1	2
Do you have feelings of dizziness or ringing in the ears?.	0	1	2
Do you crave fatty foods?	0	1	2
Do you have an excessive appetite?.	0	1	2
Does it seem difficult to strengthen your muscles?.	0	1	2
Do you have pains in the			
upper right quadrant of the stomach?	0	1	2
Is your triglyceride level above 115?	0	1	2

Total _____

Total	Recommended Dosage
0 – 14	none, Essentials For Life Only
15 – 30	1 capsule after each meal, in addition to Essentials For Life
31 – 35	2 capsules after each meal, in addition to Essentials For Life
35 - 38	3 capsules after each meal, in addition to Essentials For Life

Note: if you are trying to lose body fat, it is recommended that you take 2 capsules Lipo-chromizyme 20 minutes before exercise.

The Infinity² Nutritionals provide the foundational nutrition that every individual needs. In a month, after you have made some changes in your lifestyle by following the recommendations in this book, fill out this questionnaire again. You should find that altering your lifestyle will allow you to decrease the number of supplements you need to take. In addition to the Essential Nutritionals, you may have certain health or fitness concerns that call for additional nutrition for a short period of time.

In addition to the Essential Nutritionals, Infinity² has created additional product lines to help individuals meet any additional supplement needs they may have. The weight loss product line was developed to help individuals find a safe, natural and effective method to lose weight. The Herbals with CAᵉDS were created to provide the most effective herbs on the market. Infinity² herbs are impressive because they include the whole herb combined with CAᵉDS to ensure that your body will receive the benefits. The Sports & Conditioning line of products helps both professional and recreational athletes, as well as active individuals, meet their health and fitness goals.

If any of the statements are true for you, we recommend that you take those products along with your Infinity² Essentials for Life System.

HERBALS with CAeDS®

St. John's Wort with CAeDS®
I struggle with depression
I frequently have a feeling of hopelessness.
I struggle with emotional upsets.

Garlic with CAeDS®
I am concerned my cholesterol level is too high.
I am concerned my blood pressure is too high.
I have a family history of heart disease.

Korean Ginseng with CAeDS®
Periods of stress seem to drain my energy.
I would like to have more endurance
I need more energy to do my daily routine.

Saw Palmetto with CAeDS®
I have prostate problems, but I do not want to take a lot of drugs.
I am a male over the age of 50, and I am concerned about having prostate problems.
I am a male, and I frequently have to get up during the night to urinate.

Ginkgo Biloba with CAeDS®
I am concerned about getting Alzheimer's disease.
I don't seem to be as mentally sharp as I used to be.
As I get older, I seem to forget more important things.

Kava Kava with CAeDS®
I sometimes have difficulty getting to sleep at night.
I frequently have trouble getting "unwound" after a period of stress or excitement.
I have difficulty relaxing and would rather not take drugs.

E.N.E.R.G.Y. and Fruit Fat-Burner Bars

I want a healthy snack.

I want extra energy

I want a healthy way to satisfy my chocolate cravings.

Chapter Seven

Generates You

Chapter Seven

Generates You!

Generates

The G in the E.N.E.R.G.Y.™ acronym stands for "Generates," the perfect verb to describe what happens as you apply the principles of Envision, Nutrition, Exercise, and Replenishment. Generate means "to be the source or cause of." As you make lifestyle changes — even if they are small and gradual — this program will be the source or cause of health.

The changes that you make need not be major, overnight transformations. Instead, they can be gradual, step-by-step improvements. However, we encourage you to remember the importance of taking a wholistic approach. Make small alterations, but make alterations in each of the areas we have discussed in this book so they will all work together to generate a healthier you. Start today to:

1. **Envision health.** Find a picture of what health looks like to you and place it in a prominent place.

2. **Begin eating more nutritious meals.** For guidelines, refer to the suggestions for eating out and the many healthy recipes in this book. Also, comply with the Basics by throwing out any white flour, refined sugar, and carbonated drinks and vowing to start eating more raw foods.

3. **Exercise six days a week.** Perform the home workout three days a week, do some sort of aerobic activity on the other three days. Rest on the seventh day.

4. **Replenish the nutrients you may be missing.** Fill out the "How Much Do I Need?" questionnaire (p. 156) to determine your individual needs.

5. **Generate optimum levels of health** by sharing this message with others.

Like rolling a snowball down a hill, your commitment to health will enlarge and pick up momentum as you begin to notice the difference healthy habits can make in your life. You will have a natural inclination to share what you have learned. In fact, people will most likely ask about your newfound health.

As indicated in the "Do I Need" chapter, as you share with others, your health will reach even greater heights. Feel free to pass this book along to your family and friends or to any others you come in contact with. Remember, it will help their health and yours!

You

We have come to the last letter in the acronym. The "Y" in E.N.E.R.G.Y. represents YOU! The healthier, happier you that you envision will come about as you apply the principles outlined in this book. With that health, your most exciting dreams can come true.

We look forward to hearing about the many healthy results you achieve by following this program. You have all the principles and the tools to create optimum health, now using them is up to YOU!

Additional copies of the Complete Physique *book may be ordered from EcoQuest International, by calling 800.486.4994. If you would like information about how you can join the EcoQuest Mission of spreading healthy products to the world, call or visit www.EcoQuestIntl.com.*

Appendix

Assessment

Appendix

Assessment

An important first step in creating a vision that will draw you toward health is to determine where you are right now. Once you know where you are, you can easily monitor your progress as you learn and apply the lifestyle practices in this book. Knowing where your beginning point is will also allow you to strengthen or modify your vision when appropriate.

We recommend three important measurements for assessment:

1. Body Fat Percentage
2. Body Mass Index
3. Waist-to-Hip Ratio.

1. Body Fat Percentage

Research shows the percentage of stored body fat is directly related to health. Notice we didn't say "Weight directly affects health." Even very thin people can have a high percentage of body fat, and thus, a high risk of degenerative disease.

Most popular diet plans and many exercise programs emphasize weight loss alone. Often the low-calorie diets, meal replacement plans and improper exercise promoted as part of these plans, result in a loss of muscle, not fat.

Having a high percentage of body fat is called "a killer of major proportions" by Dr. Marc Sorenson in his book *Mega Health*. Sorenson writes: "For instance, the prevalence of hypertension is 2.9 times as high for the obese as the non-obese. Hypercholesterolemia (blood cholesterol levels over 150) is 2.1 times higher in obese people; diabetes is 2.9 times higher; cancer of the colon, rectum, prostate, gall bladder, breast, uterus and ovaries are all considerably more prevalent in the obese compared to the non-obese."

To look and feel good, to be both trim and healthy, it is important to **reduce your body fat percentage**.

For optimum health, body fat percentage for women should be between 19 and 25 percent. Men should have between 15 and 19 percent body fat.

Determine your body fat percentage, and record it on the chart provided.

Body Fat Percentages for Women

For women, to calculate your body fat percentage, you will need to use the Body Fat Percentage chart on page 175. Measure your hips, your abdomen and your height, then follow the computation formula below. As mentioned earlier, for optimum health, the average women should have between 19 to 25 percent body fat.

Computation

Hips   (in inches) _____   =   Constant A _____

Height   (in inches) _____   =   Constant C _____

Abdomen   (in inches) _____   =   Constant B _____

Constants A plus B =   _____

minus Constant C   _____

Equals   _____%   **(Percent Body Fat)**

Body Fat Percentages for Men

For men, measure your waist and wrist, and then weigh yourself. Subtract your wrist measurement from your waist measurement. Then use this sum, along with your weight, to determine your body fat percentage according to the charts on pages 176-178.

As mentioned earlier, men should have between 15 and 19 percent body fat.

2. Body Mass Index

Another valuable measurement is called the body mass index (BMI) which incorporates both height and weight to assess a person's level of fatness.

According to the June 1993 *Consumer's Report*, scientists say:

BMI of 25 or less — desirable for most people.

BMI between 25 and 30 — mild or moderately overweight — Slightly

increased risk of weight-related health problems such as high blood pressure,

high blood cholesterol, heart disease, and Type II (adult-onset) diabetes.

BMI of 30 or more — considered truly overweight — The risk of developing
the above conditions and others rises sharply.

Determine your BMI and record it below.

Finding your BMI

Calculate your BMI as follows: Multiply your weight in pounds by 700, divide by your height in inches, then divide by your height again.

Weight (in pounds)   _____

                      x   700

                      =   _____

Height (in inches)   ÷   _____

                      =   _____

Height (in inches)   ÷   _____

           BMI   =   _____

3. Waist-to-Hip Ratio

Your waist-to-hip ratio is another way to gauge your health. The waist-to-hip ratio is the measurement of a person's waist at its smallest point, divided by the circumference of the hips at their widest point.

This ratio distinguishes "apples" — that is, people who carry excess weight above their waist — from "pears" — people whose extra fat settles around the hips and buttocks. Studies show that the higher the waist-to-hip ratio, the more apple-shaped the figure and the greater the risk of disease.

Cardiovascular disease has been linked to waist-to-hip ratio in several long-term studies. For men, the risk seems to rise if the waist-to-hip ratio is above 0.95; for women, the risk increases at 0.80.

Abdominal fat is also associated with increased insulin resistance (a precursor to diabetes) and may be a cause of hypertension.

Most men are "apples," and often have the classic "beer belly," and most women are "pears." Studies show that men are much less likely to try to lose weight, so they are often at a higher risk than women.

Determine your waist-to-hip ratio and record it in the spaces that follow.

To calculate your waist-to-hip ratio:

Using a tape measure, find the circumference of your waist at its narrowest point when your stomach is relaxed.

      Waist: _____ in.

Next, measure the circumference of your hips at their widest point (where your buttocks protrude the most).

      Hips: _____ in.

Finally, divide your waist measurement by your hip measurement.

      Waist divided by hips = _____ **Waist-to-hip ratio**

Yardstick of Health

Use these three measurements: body fat percentage, body mass index and waist-to-hip ratio, as a yardstick of health.

Compare the measurements you have recorded on your chart with the recommended ranges listed above. Use these comparisons to determine which areas need improvement, so you can formulate a clear vision of what you want to accomplish.

If it looks like you have a long way to go, don't be discouraged, you will soon notice changes! Put these measurements away and use your positive mental images to help you create health. Regard this assessment only as a first step and a way to get started in the right direction. After you have been following the recommendations in *Complete Physique* for six weeks, calculate these measurements again, and celebrate the improvements!

Body Fat Percentages for Women

Hips			Abdomen			Height	
In.	Constant A		In.	Constant B		In.	Constant C
30	33.48		20	14.22		55	33.52
31	34.87		21	14.93		56	34.13
32	36.27		22	15.64		57	34.74
33	36.67		23	16.35		58	35.35
34	39.06		24	17.06		59	35.96
35	40.46		25	17.78		60	36.57
36	41.86		26	18.49		61	37.18
37	43.25		27	19.20		62	37.79
38	44.65		28	19.91		63	38.40
39	46.05		29	20.62		64	39.01
40	47.44		30	21.33		65	39.62
41	48.84		31	22.04		66	40.23
42	50.24		32	22.75		67	40.84
43	51.64		33	23.46		68	41.45
44	53.03		34	24.18		69	42.06
45	54.43		35	24.89		70	42.67
46	55.83		36	25.60		71	43.28
47	57.22		37	26.31		72	43.89
48	58.62		38	27.02		73	44.50
49	60.02		39	27.73		74	45.11
50	61.42		40	28.44		75	45.72
51	62.81		41	29.15		76	46.32
52	64.21		42	29.87		77	46.93
53	65.61		43	30.58		78	47.54
54	67.00		44	31.29		79	48.15
55	68.40		45	32.00		80	48.76
56	69.80		46	32.71		81	49.37
57	71.19		47	33.42		82	49.98
58	72.59		48	34.13		83	50.59
59	73.99		49	34.84		84	51.20
60	75.39		50	35.56		85	51.81

A= _____   B= _____   C= _____

Body Fat Percentages for Men

Waist Minus Wrist

Wt.	22	22.5	23	23.5	24	24.5	25	25.5	26	26.5	27	27.5	28	28.5	29	29.5	30	30.5	31
120	4	6	8	10	12	14	16	18	20	21	23	25	27	29	31	33	35	37	39
125	4	6	7	9	11	13	15	17	19	20	22	24	26	28	30	32	33	35	37
130	3	5	7	9	11	12	14	16	18	20	21	23	25	27	28	30	32	34	36
135	3	5	7	8	10	12	13	15	17	19	20	22	24	26	27	29	31	32	34
140	3	5	6	8	10	11	13	15	16	18	19	21	23	24	26	28	29	31	33
145	3	4	6	7	9	11	12	14	15	17	18	20	22	23	25	27	28	30	31
150	2	4	6	7	9	10	12	13	14	16	17	19	21	23	24	26	27	29	30
155	2	3	5	7	8	10	11	13	13	16	16	19	20	22	23	25	26	28	29
160	2	3	5	6	8	9	10	12	13	15	16	17	19	20	22	23	24	26	27
165	2	3	5	6	8	9	10	12	13	15	15	17	18	20	22	23	24	26	27
170	2	3	4	6	7	9	10	11	12	14	15	16	17	19	21	22	23	25	26
175	2	3	4	6	7	8	9	11	12	13	14	16	17	19	20	21	22	24	25
180	1	3	4	5	7	8	9	10	11	13	13	15	16	18	19	21	22	23	25
185	1	2	4	5	6	8	8	10	11	13	13	15	16	18	19	20	21	23	24
190	1	2	4	5	6	7	8	10	11	12	12	14	15	17	18	19	21	22	23
195	1	2	3	4	6	7	8	9	11	12	12	14	15	16	18	19	20	21	22
200	1	2	3	4	5	7	7	9	10	11	11	13	14	16	17	18	19	21	22
205	1	2	3	4	5	6	7	9	10	11	11	13	14	15	17	18	19	20	22
210	1	2	3	4	5	6	7	8	9	11	11	12	13	15	16	17	18	19	21
215	1	2	3	4	4	6	6	8	9	10	10	12	13	14	16	17	18	19	21
220	1	1	3	3	4	6	6	8	9	10	10	12	12	14	15	16	17	18	20
225	0	1	3	3	4	5	6	7	9	10	9	11	12	13	15	16	17	18	19
230	0	1	2	3	4	5	6	7	8	9	9	11	12	13	14	15	16	17	19
235	0	1	2	3	4	5	5	7	8	9	9	11	11	13	14	15	16	17	18
240	0	1	2	3	4	5	5	7	8	9	9	10	11	12	14	15	16	16	18
245	0	1	2	3	4	5	5	6	7	9	8	10	10	12	13	14	15	16	17
250	0	1	2	3	4	5	5	6	7	8	8	10	10	12	13	14	15	15	17
255	0	1	2	3	3	4	5	6	7	8	8	10	10	12	13	14	14	15	17
260	0	1	2	2	3	4	4	6	7	8	8	9	10	11	12	13	14	15	16
265	0	1	2	2	3	4	4	6	6	8	8	9	9	11	12	13	14	14	16
270	0	0	1	2	3	4	4	5	6	7	7	9	9	11	12	13	13	14	15
275	0	0	1	2	3	4	4	5	6	7	7	8	9	11	12	13	13	14	15
280	0	0	1	2	3	4	4	5	6	7	7	8	9	10	11	12	13	13	15
285	0	0	1	2	3	3	4	5	6	7	7	8	9	10	11	12	12	13	14
290	0	0	1	2	2	3	4	5	6	7	7	8	9	10	11	11	12	13	14
295	0	0	1	2	2	3	4	5	6	6	7	8	9	10	11	11	12	13	14
300	0	0	1	2	2	3	4	5	5	6	7	8	9	9	10	11	12	12	13

Body Fat Percentages for Men

Wt.	Waist Minus Wrist																		
	31.5	32	32.5	33	33.5	34	34.5	35	35.5	36	36.5	37	37.5	38	38.5	39	39.5	40	40.5
120	40	43	45	47	49	50	52	54	56	58	60	62	64	66	68	70	72	74	76
125	39	41	43	45	46	48	50	52	54	56	58	59	61	63	65	67	69	71	72
130	37	39	41	43	44	46	48	50	52	53	55	57	59	61	62	64	66	68	69
135	36	38	39	41	43	44	46	48	50	51	53	55	56	58	60	62	63	65	67
140	34	36	38	39	41	43	44	46	48	49	51	53	54	56	58	59	61	63	64
145	33	35	36	38	40	41	43	44	46	47	49	51	52	54	55	57	59	60	62
150	32	33	35	36	38	40	41	43	44	46	47	49	50	52	53	55	57	58	60
155	31	32	34	35	37	38	40	41	43	44	46	47	49	50	52	53	55	56	58
160	30	31	33	34	36	37	38	40	41	43	44	46	47	48	50	51	53	54	56
165	29	30	31	33	34	36	37	38	40	41	43	44	45	47	48	50	51	52	54
170	28	29	30	32	33	34	36	37	39	40	41	43	44	45	47	48	49	51	52
175	27	28	29	31	32	33	35	36	37	39	40	41	43	44	45	47	48	49	51
180	26	27	28	30	31	32	34	35	36	38	39	40	41	43	44	45	47	48	49
185	25	26	28	29	30	31	33	34	35	36	38	39	40	41	43	44	45	46	48
190	24	26	27	28	29	30	32	33	34	35	37	38	39	40	41	43	44	45	46
195	24	25	26	27	28	30	31	32	33	34	35	37	38	39	40	41	43	44	45
200	23	24	25	26	28	29	30	31	32	33	35	36	37	38	39	40	41	43	44
205	22	23	25	26	27	28	29	30	31	32	34	35	36	37	38	39	40	41	43
210	22	23	24	25	26	27	28	29	30	32	33	34	35	36	37	38	39	40	42
215	21	22	23	24	25	26	28	29	30	31	32	33	34	35	36	37	38	39	40
220	20	22	23	24	25	26	27	28	29	30	31	32	33	34	35	36	37	38	39
225	20	21	23	24	26	25	26	27	28	29	30	31	32	33	34	35	36	37	38
230	19	21	22	23	23	24	25	26	27	28	30	31	32	33	34	35	36	37	38
235	19	20	21	22	23	24	24	26	27	28	29	30	31	32	33	34	35	36	37
240	18	19	20	21	22	23	24	25	26	27	28	29	30	31	32	33	34	35	36
245	18	19	20	21	22	23	23	25	26	27	27	28	29	30	31	32	33	34	35
250	18	18	19	20	21	22	23	24	25	26	27	28	29	30	31	31	32	33	34
255	17	18	19	20	21	22	23	24	24	25	26	27	28	30	30	31	32	33	34
260	17	18	19	19	20	21	23	23	24	25	26	27	27	28	29	30	31	32	33
265	16	17	18	19	20	21	22	22	23	24	25	26	27	28	29	29	30	31	32
270	16	17	18	19	19	20	21	22	23	24	25	25	26	27	28	29	30	31	31
275	16	16	17	18	19	19	20	21	22	23	24	25	26	26	27	28	29	30	31
280	15	16	17	18	18	19	20	21	21	22	23	24	25	26	26	27	28	29	30
285	15	16	16	17	18	19	19	20	21	22	23	23	24	25	26	27	27	28	29
290	14	15	16	17	17	18	19	20	21	21	22	23	24	25	25	26	27	28	28
295	14	15	16	16	17	18	19	19	20	21	22	22	23	24	25	26	26	27	28
300	14	15	16	16	17	18	19	19	20	21	22	22	23	24	25	26	26	27	28

Body Fat Percentages for Men

Waist Minus Wrist

Wt.	41	41.5	42	42.5	43	43.5	44	44.5	45	45.5	46	46.5	47	47.5	48	48.5	49	49.5	50
120	77	79	81	83	85	87	89	91	93	95	97	99	99	99	99	99	99	99	99
125	74	76	78	80	82	84	85	87	89	91	93	95	96	98	99	99	99	99	99
130	71	73	75	77	78	80	82	84	86	87	89	91	93	94	96	98	99	99	99
135	68	70	72	74	75	77	79	80	82	84	86	87	89	91	92	94	96	98	99
140	66	68	69	71	72	74	76	77	79	81	82	84	86	87	89	91	92	94	96
145	63	65	67	68	70	71	73	75	76	78	79	81	83	84	86	87	89	91	92
150	61	63	64	66	67	69	70	72	74	75	77	78	80	81	83	84	86	87	89
155	59	61	62	64	65	67	68	70	71	73	74	76	77	79	80	82	83	85	86
160	57	59	60	61	63	64	66	67	69	70	72	73	75	76	77	79	80	82	83
165	55	57	58	60	61	62	64	65	67	68	69	71	72	74	75	76	78	79	81
170	54	55	56	58	59	60	62	63	64	66	67	69	70	71	73	74	75	77	78
175	52	53	55	56	57	59	60	61	63	64	65	66	68	69	70	72	73	74	76
180	50	52	53	54	56	57	58	59	61	62	63	65	66	67	68	70	71	72	74
185	49	50	51	53	54	55	56	58	59	60	61	63	64	65	66	68	69	70	71
190	48	49	50	51	52	54	55	56	57	58	60	61	62	63	65	66	67	68	69
195	46	47	49	50	51	52	53	55	56	57	58	59	60	62	63	64	65	66	68
200	45	46	47	48	50	51	52	53	54	55	57	58	59	60	61	62	63	65	66
205	44	45	46	47	48	49	51	52	53	54	55	56	57	58	60	61	62	63	64
210	43	44	45	46	47	48	49	50	51	53	54	55	56	57	58	59	60	61	62
215	42	43	44	45	46	47	48	49	50	51	52	53	54	56	57	58	59	60	61
220	41	42	43	44	45	46	47	48	49	50	51	52	53	54	55	56	57	58	59
225	40	41	42	43	44	45	46	47	48	49	50	51	52	53	54	55	56	57	58
230	39	40	41	42	43	44	45	46	47	48	49	50	51	52	53	54	55	56	57
235	38	39	40	41	42	43	44	45	46	47	48	49	50	51	51	52	53	54	55
240	37	38	39	40	41	42	43	44	45	46	46	47	48	49	50	51	52	53	54
245	36	37	38	39	40	41	42	43	44	44	45	46	47	48	49	50	51	52	53
250	35	36	37	38	39	40	41	42	43	44	44	45	46	47	48	49	50	51	52
255	34	35	36	37	38	39	40	41	42	43	44	44	45	46	47	48	49	50	51
260	34	35	35	36	37	38	39	40	41	42	43	43	44	45	46	47	48	49	50
265	33	34	35	36	36	37	38	39	40	41	42	43	43	44	45	46	47	48	49
270	32	33	34	35	36	37	37	38	39	40	41	42	43	43	44	45	46	47	48
275	32	32	33	34	35	36	37	37	38	39	40	41	42	43	44	44	45	46	47
280	31	32	33	33	34	35	37	37	38	38	39	40	41	42	43	43	45	45	46
285	30	31	32	33	34	34	35	36	37	38	39	39	40	41	42	43	43	44	45
290	30	31	31	32	33	34	35	35	36	37	38	39	39	40	41	42	43	43	44
295	29	30	31	32	32	33	34	35	36	36	37	38	39	39	40	41	42	43	43
300	29	29	30	31	32	33	33	34	35	36	36	37	38	39	39	40	41	42	43

References

Chapter Two - Do I Need?

1. Burros, Marian. "Additives in Advice on Food?" *New York Times*, Nov. 15, 1995, vol. 145 p. C1.

2. Fallon, Sally and Mary G. Enig, PhD. "Diet and Heart Disease: Not What You Think." *Consumers' Research*, July 1996, p.19.

3. Jocelyn Elders; NNFA Convention, March 1995, Report in Anaheim, CA.

4. U.S. Department of Commerce, Economics and Statistics Administration; Bureau of the Census. An Aging World II: International Population Reports - P95/92-3.

5. Suinn. *Self-Directed Behavior*. 1976.

6. Dossey, Larry, M.D. *Meaning and Medicine*. New York: Bantam Books, 1991, p. 172.

7. *Surgeon General's Report on Nutrition and Health*. U.S. Department of Health and Human Services, Centers for Disease Control and Prevention, National Center for Chronic Disease Prevention and Health Promotion; 1988.

8. Pottenger, Francis M., Jr., M.D. *Pottenger's Cats: A Study in Nutrition*. p. 9.

9. *Ibid.*, p. 45.

10. *Ibid.*, p. 81.

11. Pao, Eleanor M. and Sharon J. Mickle. "Nutrients from meals and snacks consumed by individuals." Family Economics Review, U.S. Department of Agriculture, Science and Administration, Beltsville, MD.

12. Lee, Royal, D.D.S. "Land, Health and Politics"

13. Lee, Royal, D.D.S. "The Missing Nutritional Elements"

14. Fallon, *op. cit.*

15. Burros, Marian, *op cit.*

16. Ten-State Nutrition Survey, DHEW Publ. No. (HSM) 72-8130-8134, U.S. Department of Health, Education and Welfare, Health Serviced and Mental Health Administration Center for Disease Control, Atlanta, GA.

17. Drexler, Madeline. "Ten Reasons Why It's Hard to Change our Eating Habits (and three reasons why we might)." *The Boston Globe Magazine*, July 21, 1996, p.16.

18. Krehl, Willard A., "The Role of Nutrition in Preventing Diseases." Speech presented at Davidson Conference Center for Continuing Education, University of Southern California School of Dentistry, February 29, 1981.

19. U.S. Department of Health and Human Services. *Physical Activity and Health: A Report of the Surgeon General*. Atlanta, GA: U.S. Department of Helath and Human Services, Centers for Disease Control and Prevention, National Center for Chronic Disease Prevention and Health Promotion, 1996, p. 4.

20. The Center for Disease Control. "Progress toward achieving the 1990 national objectives for physical fitness and exercise." MMWR 1989; 38:449-453.

21. U.S. Department of Health and Human Services, *op. cit.*

22. Blair, S. "Physical Fitness and all causes of mortality. A prospective study of healthy men and women." *Journal of the American Medical Association*. 1989, 262: 2395-2401.

23. *Ibid.*

24. U.S. Department of Health and Human Services, *op. cit.*

25. *Ibid.*

26. Henig, Robin Marantz. "The Great Diet Scam," *Self*. December 1992, p. 70 and "Losing Weight: What Works, What Doesn't," *Consumers' Report*, June 1993, p. 353.

27. Westcott, Wayne. *Strength Fitness: Physiological Principles and Training Techniques*. W. C. Brown Publishers: Dubuque, IA, 1989; p. xiii.

28. *Ibid.* p. 1.

29. Newmark, Gretchen Rose, M.A., R.D. and James M. Gerber, M.S., D.C. "Antioxidants — Key to a Healthier Life," *Let's Live*, November, 1992.

30. "Composition of Foods." Agriculture Handbook No. 8, U.S. Department of Agriculture.

31. Luks, Allan, "Helper's High," *Psychology Today*, October 1988, pp. 39-42.

32. Dossey, Larry, M.D., *op. cit.*

33. Moyers, Bill. *Healing and the Mind*. New York: Doubleday, 1993, p. 216.

Chapter Three - Envision

1. Chopra, Deepak, M.D. *Creating Health: How to Wake Up the Body's Intelligence.* Boston: Houghton Mifflin Company, 1991, p. 97.

2. Maltz, Maxwell, M.D., F.I.C.S.. *Psycho-cybernetics: A New Way to Get More Living Out of Life.* New York: Simon and Schuster, Inc., 1960, p. 31.

3. *Ibid.*, p. 32.

4. Deaton, Dennis R. *The Book on Mind Management.* Mesa, Arizona: MMI Publishing, 1994.

5. *Ibid.*

6. Maltz, *op. cit.*

Chapter Four - Nutrition

1. *Surgeon General's Report on Nutrition and Health.* U.S. Department of Health and Human Services, Centers for Disease Control and Prevention, National Center for Chronic Disease Prevention and Health Promotion; 1988.

2. *Ibid.*

Chapter Five - Exercise

1. Anderson, Bob, Bill Pearl and Edmund R. Burke, Ph. D. *Getting in Shape: Workout Programs for Men and Women.* Bolinas, California: Shelter Publications, 1994, p. 142.

2. Westcott, Wayne. *Strength Fitness: Physiological Principles and Training Techniques.* W. C. Brown Publishers: Dubuque, IA, 1989.

3. *Ibid.*

4. Evans, William. "Delaying the Aging Process." *Nutrition Action Healthletter.* Vol. 22, No. 10. December 1995, p. 5.

5. U.S. Department of Health and Human Services. *Physical Activity and Health: A Report of the Surgeon General.* Atlanta, GA: U.S. Department of Helath and Human Services, Centers for Disease Control and Prevention, National Center for Chronic Disease Prevention and Health Promotion, 1996, p. 6.

6. *Ibid.*

7. NFPT Review. February/March 1995.

8. U.S. Department of Health and Human Services. *op. cit.*

9. *Ibid.*

Chapter Six - Replenishment

1. U.S. Department of Agriculture Study, 1982.

2. Kautchakoff, Paul, M.D. "The Influence of Food Cooking on the Blood Formula of Man," Lausanne, Switzerland, 1930.

3. Howell, Edward. *Enzyme Nutrition.* Wayne, New Jersey: Avery Publishing Group, Inc.

4. *Ibid.*

5. Shahani, Khem M. "The Role of Probiotics in Gastrointestinal Microecology, Health and Disease," presented at the seminar on Multiple Modalities of Orthomolecular and Nutritional Medicine. 1993.

6. Bynum, Stan. "The Plague of the 21st Century" Live seminar presentation at Infinity², January, 1997.

7. "Warning: Antibiotics Could Endanger Your Child." *Reader's Digest,* December 1996, p. 113-7.

8. "Maintaining Intestinal Flora Through Probiotics," *op. cit.*

9. Gorner, Peter and Ronald Kotulak. "Scientists try to tame molecular 'sharks'." *Chicago Tribune,* Wednesday December 11, 1991. Front page.

10. Reuben, Carolyn. *Antioxidants: Your Complete Guide.* Rocklin, CA: Prima Publishing, 1995, p. 8.

11. *Ibid.*

12. National Center for Health Statistics. An epidemic of obesity. Newsweek 1 Aug. 1994, p 62.

13. Hird National Health and Nutrition Examination Survey," The University of California Berkeley Wellness Letter, Feb. 1994.

14. Kuczmarsk RJ et al. Varying body mass index cutoff points to describe overweight prevalence among U.S. adults: NHANES III (1988 to 1994). Obes. Res. 1997; 5:542-548.

15. Calle EE et al. Body mass index and mortality in prospective cohort of U.S. adults. New England Journal of Medicine 1999; 341(15):1097-1105.

16. Gutman RA et al. Long-term hypertriglyceridemia and glucose intolerance in rats fed chronically an isocaloric sucrose-rich diet. Metab. Clin. Exp. 1987; 36:1013-1020.

17. Anderson RA and Kozlovsky AJ. Am J Clin Nutr 1985; 41:1177-1183.

18. Davis CM and Vincent JB. Chromium in carbohydrate and lipid metabolism. J Biol Inorg Chem 1997; 2:675-579.

19. Stearns DM et al. Chromium (III) picolinate produces chromosome damage in Chinese hamster ovary cells. FASEB J 1995; 9:1643-1648.

Stock Numbers

U.S. STOCK #	DESCRIPTION
INFINITY² ESSENTIALS FOR LIFE	
69600	Infinity² Essentials For Life System (Two bottle system, 90 Capsules per bottle)
NUTRITIONAL LINE	
69603	Insure Plus (90 count)
69604	Digest-a-Meal (90 count)
69605	Lipo-chromizyme (90 count)
69608	Chelated Mineral Complex (90 count)
69606	Life Force Super Antioxidant (60 count)
69607	Total Flora Support (90 count)
	- Complete Physique (book only)
HERBS WITH CAEDS	
69612	Korean Ginseng with CA^{e}DS (60 count)
69617	St. John's Wort with CA^{e}DS (60 count)
69613	Echinacea with CA^{e}DS (60 count)
69611	Garlic with CA^{e}DS (60 count)
69618	Kava Kava with CA^{e}DS (60 count)
69614	Saw Palmetto with CA^{e}DS (60 count)
69615	Ginkgo Biloba with CA^{e}DS (60 count)
SPORTS & CONDITIONING LINE	
69609	E.N.E.R.G.Y. Bar (20 count)
69610	Fruit Fat-Burner Bar (20 count)

ORDER ONLINE @

www.EcoQuestIntl.com

PHONE ORDERS:

1.800.486.4994

Fax 423.638.7561